BREAK UP,
DON'T BREAK DOWN

*A relationship manual for surviving breakups,
separation, and divorce.*

D. Ivan Young

Reality -N- 3D Publishing, Inc.

Break Up, Don't Break Down
A relationship manual for surviving breakups, separation, and divorce.
by D. Ivan Young

Reality -N- 3D Publishing, Inc.
P.O. Box 509
Houston, TX 77001

ISBN: 978 -0-9665132-0-2
Library of Congress Control Number 2010902745

To my adopted parents, the late Cicero and Juanita Young, and to my mother, Helen Rose Robinson.

Thank you, God, for seeing me through!

CONTENTS

INTRODUCTION

Break Up, Don't Break Down provides a road map for anyone who's trapped by the past anger, guilt and pressures of a failed relationship. Here you'll find ten steps to happiness despite your breakup. This user-friendly manual is designed to show you how to get past the pain, stress and disappointment that come from breaking up, and to move you past the hurt and pain caused by a broken love affair.

Chapter by chapter, you will find a simple, direct, uncomplicated discussion of issues that range from ending the dysfunctional relationship to dealing with guilt or peer pressure, minimizing the negative effects on your children, creating a new life and finding new love.

It doesn't matter if you have a PhD or a GED, I tell it like it is, using down-to-earth language. Go ahead and take a break from your therapist, stop calling and worrying your friends, wipe the tears away. *Break Up, Don't Break Down* will help you get over the pain of a dying relationship and show you how to get on with rest of your life.

Use *Break Up, Don't Break Down* as a tool to end what used to be a relationship. It's not a feel-good book; this is a relationship manual created to guide you through the breakup process. When crying, and talking to friends and relatives doesn't ease the pain, this book serves as a supportive, non-judgmental companion. It contains everything you need to ease you through the breaking up, separation or divorce. Using, wisdom, sound logic, faith and proven relationship strategies, *Break Up, Don't Break Down* is filled with the information and the motivation you need to successfully deal with the separation and ultimate healing from a destructive, abusive or unhealthy relationship. No longer will you be left feeling helpless.

Contained within are:

- Emotional survival skills
- Dealing with pain and guilt
- Helping children adjust to separation or divorce
- Help with loneliness
- Establishing a new identity
- Skills that teach you how to resuscitate your life
- Creating a new life plan
- How to find and keep quality people in your life
- Finding, keeping and understanding love
- Getting rid of emotional baggage
- Cleaning up self-destructive thoughts
- Finding, meeting and keeping the love of your life

Chances are, that relationship you're ending has been knocking at death's door for quite some time now or should never have begun to start with. The handwriting has been on the wall but you didn't have the courage to say that it's over. Bad advice from your peers, relatives and so-called friends is more than likely all, or at least part, of the reason you haven't had the courage to let go and get on with your life. Your family and friends may have no clue of the stress and extreme pain you suffer on a daily basis or they may not know any different themselves. Remember, misery loves company.

Many people prolong dissolution because they just don't want to deal with confrontation. That is the equivalent of being too tired to take a bath because the longer you wait the more life stinks. If you're reading this, that's proof it's time to break away from the pack. You will have to do this on your own and you can!

No one in their right mind sets out in life to fail at anything, especially if it results in a broken heart. It doesn't matter whose fault it is—it hurts the same. Relationships end for different reasons. Often people grow apart. At times there's infidelity or disloyalty. Whatever the case, as with all things in life eventually even the best of situations are subject to what seems to be a heartless end. Be it karma, poor judgement, immaturity or just plain stupid moves, all bad relationships end because they weren't established properly from the start. Now, before you go blaming someone else, examine your contribution to the situation. God promised you life, not misery, and life more abundantly. He also feeds the birds every day but he doesn't throw worms in the nest or help them build it. Only a fool begins construction of anything from a nest to a house to a relationship without first planning and examining its cost. Remember this: Anything built on an unsteady foundation will fall.

VALUE YOUR TIME

Time cannot be replaced and you don't have any more time to waste. Everything in creation that has significant value is measured in seconds, minutes, days, weeks, months, and years. Wasting that precious time is foolish and consequential. It's easy to replace things, to recover lost money, even opportunity, but the one thing in life that you cannot get back in life is time. So rejoice in the fact that you are finally strong enough to accept the truth. This relationship has run its course and it's time for it to be over. It's over now!

Love suffers long, but only a fool suffers forever. Outsiders may say it is hard to believe; what they thought would stand the test of time, the relationship which you invested so much in and truly believed God must have joined, has come to an end. In spite of it all, your life must go on. You can't open yourself to God's future gifts if you hang onto what you settled for or gave yourself. Mediocrity is the worst of the best and the best of the worst.

Beloved, I want you to rest assured, you're not the first, and you won't be the last person to go through the stress, pain and heartache of breaking up. As bad as that sounds, I want you to be encouraged. What is meant to curse you will bless you. Your relationship may be 'breaking up,' but you will not be 'breaking down.' If anything, you're correcting a mistake that was hurting four people, you and the person you're with, not to mention the two people who you were destined to meet.

Bleak as things may appear, you deserve to be loved and this time we are going to make sure it is by the right person, even if the someone who's loving you is yourself. Let's take baby steps. Begin by being thankful for everything that's right in your life. Start with that good friend or close relative (this includes that play brother or sister), co-worker or even a casual acquaintance who sees enough value in you to let you know that you deserve better. That's right. You're entitled to much more than what you have been settling for. Even if that good friend is just that little voice inside you, that's all the better.

Most good people experience extreme fear, depression, sadness, anger and guilt as they attempt to withdraw from a hurtful or dysfunctional situation. The worst part is that people trapped in such circumstances don't have a clue how they ended up there. Making matters worse, they are often afraid to cause hurt feelings or are too embarrassed or even scared to leave. After weeks, months or years of putting up with a non-productive relationship most individuals have been sapped of any faith, hope or self-esteem they had left. This is directly attributed to the fact that much of it has been drained by what we are going to call 'the love parasite.' If you are sick and tired of seeing yourself or someone you care deeply about going through a situation like this, then *Break Up, Don't Break Down* is written for you.

This book winding up in your hands isn't an accident. Whether you were searching the Internet, browsing through the bookstore, or someone handed you this book, it's not a mere coincidence. God answers prayers when you need Him most. It is not accidental; it is part of your destiny. There is such a thing as divine intervention. The fact that it's taking place right now is proof. Heaven knows when to give you the help you desperately need. As a mother hears the cry of her infant, the universe is sensitive to what's going on with your life.

As an author and life coach, my job is rescuing and resurrecting people who are hurting from inappropriate, hopeless and broken situations. That which you seek is equally seeking you. God gets sick and tired of your not maximizing your day.

Take a moment to reflect over the past several weeks, months and, for some of you, years. How often did and do you hear yourself making statements like this: 'What the hell am I doing in this situation? Every day this gets worse and worse. Why am I putting up with this? I'm sick and tired, I'll be so glad when this mess is finally over. I can't take it anymore. This is cool, but something just isn't right.' FYI: That's your spirit talking; don't you think it's time that you listen?

I can assure you that from this moment forward, things are going to change for the better. For transformation to happen, you must summon the courage to leave the lesser-known for the greater unknown. Believe me, I know you may feel alone or uneasy but know that you're not by yourself. Breakups, separations, and even divorce happen to many people who never dreamed they would be in this situation. None of us is immune from experiencing the pain that comes as a result of a failed relationship. It does not matter how much money you have, how much education you've attained, what your zip code is, how long your mom and daddy stayed married, how much you spent on your wedding. Race, gender, religion, not even your age—not one of these things exempts you from pain. The good news is that this is not the end of the world. In many instances it is the beginning.

LEARN FROM THE PAST

However, to prevent the same thing from happening in the future, we must examine the mistakes of today. We're going to begin the process by doing an autopsy on the remains of this love affair. In the end, it doesn't matter who or what caused the collapse. You still have some stress, chaos and a mess. Be encouraged. With a little work, we're going to turn this curse into a blessing.

Wise people take the time to examine why, what and how things happen in life; they don't accept mediocrity and negativity as the status quo. It's time that you take a good

7

look at the circumstances that you have allowed to stifle the last few weeks, months or possibly years of your life. How fair are you being to yourself or the person you're with? Is it fair that you're sanctioning someone else to hinder your future or interfere with your hopes and dreams? Or, are you enabling that person to cripple the things that you've birthed, only to have your dreams end up in a gloomy, pessimistic, dying environment?

You are not a failure, nor have you failed because this relationship didn't work. It's time to stop the pity party and salvage the priceless time that's left in your life. Be you twenty-one or sixty-one, life is too short and death is too long to take time for granted. Grow up, accept the fact that some things in life reach a point where they are simply beyond repair or should have never happened in the first place. Don't get down on yourself. Healing is never an easy process.

Take comfort: you are not a loser. Love, like life, is not fair but it is just. When nurtured, love thrives; however, when taken for granted, love dies. Life is full of painful and difficult lessons. The trick is converting a difficult lesson into a marvelous blessing. One of life's hardest lessons is that love doesn't love anybody. Love is a power and success with it comes by respecting love's capacity to transform your life for the better or for worse. Passion is the only game that two people can play and both lose. Remember this: Whether you're the person who's getting dumped or the one that's doing the dumping, you can move on to create a new and successful relationship. To paraphrase a common truth: One person's trash—or trashed relationship—is another's treasure.

It's time to stop settling for less than you deserve from life. How many times are you going to allow someone to call you something other than your name, especially if that someone is you? It's difficult enough to deal with the problems of normal life everyday, let alone attempt to handle with these strains while suffering mistreatment at the hands of those who should love you—that includes your not loving and respecting others or yourself—or being in the right relationship with the wrong person. Mankind was given dominion over the birds of the air, the beasts of the field, the fish of the sea, and the things that passed through the air and the seas. I do not recall hearing anything about man being given dominion over other people. In other words, the only person you can control is you!

Once upon a time, I heard a wise man say, 'Common sense is the cause of many good relationships; likewise, a lack of common sense results in many bad ones.' You can dress up a mule, board it with thoroughbreds, groom it, give it the best trainer, but at the end of the day you still have a jackass. Few people possess the courage to quit while they're ahead. Do you process such courage? One can liken this to becoming lost while driving. The sooner you turn around and get on the right track the better off you are.

MOVE FORWARD

Though we have a long way to go, congratulate yourself that you have taken the first step on a wonderful journey called the rest of your life. What you're doing takes courage and nerve. Weak people cannot speak up, let alone stand up for themselves. The mere fact that you are taking this first step is evidence you are neither helpless nor weak. You're on your way to becoming what God intended you to be. Be proud of yourself and convinced that you can succeed. Transformation requires faith in God and yourself. Remember: faith without works is dead, so, let's do the work. Begin by admitting that you need to rid yourself of an unhealthy situation.

Now, you've taken the first step toward wholeness. It's the season to remember who you are. Moreover, I want you to become reacquainted with the real you. Equally important, I want you to take a stand on who you are not. You're not what you have become; you're not the negative things that others say about you. What you have done in the past might have been foolish, but what you're doing right now proves you are not a fool. You're in command of your destiny and your life is not out of control. Beneath all of this mess you're still the person God created you to be. Let's get ready to take authority over your life. It is your time.

I wrote this book, designed the workbook and created the CDs that accompany it for one reason, to empower you. I sincerely believe that you deserve to get the love, joy, peace and happiness back into your life with the right person. This process begins with learning to love yourself and all that constitutes the life that God destined for you. This may be the beginning, the middle, or end of a break up, but you will not break down.

By the time this book is finished, you and I will have perfected your communication skills. You are going to hear the voice of your inner being, that is, the Holy Spirit inside you. What matters most is that you listen to the divine part of yourself; this is the moment when you realize that it doesn't matter who acted as a spark plug for getting this tool in your hand. Now is the time and the season for you to get out of this mess.

You are somebody special. Despite what you're going through at the moment, know that God has a wonderful plan for the rest of your life. Eyes have not seen, nor ears heard, neither has it entered into the hearts of men the goodness that awaits you. Although weeping may endure for a night, joy comes in the morning. A home is supposed to be a sanctuary, not a mortuary. So it's time to stop clenching your teeth, having heart palpitations, taking deep breaths on your way to your own house. Life without love is nothing. It's time to choose a better life, filled with love. You deserve it. Today, right now, this very moment, is the beginning of the rest of your life.

As with many things in life, transition is not the end, but the beginning. It's normal that you wonder, why, why did this happen to me? After we've done all that we can do, sometimes our best simply is not good enough. But, that's okay. Cry your last cry, try your last try, and give all you have to give; now it's okay to be officially through because enough is enough!

This is the end of the pity party. We've reached the last 'why me?' Today—yes, today—ask yourself another question: 'Why not me?'

CHAPTER 1

IT'S OVER. IT'S OVER NOW.

ENDING YOUR RELATIONSHIP

I am not attempting to be funny, but once I attended a funeral that lasted so long, I began wishing I were dead. It made absolutely no sense to take that long to lay a dead man to rest. My cousin went outside, smoked a cigarette, drank a Coke, and came back. The church had no air conditioning. Even the deceased started sweating. I remember saying, 'If they don't hurry up and finish this, I'm going to roll the damn man outside and bury him myself. For crying out loud, the man is dead, let's pay our respects and go before someone else drops dead from fatigue or boredom.' My point is: Sometimes we have to know when to let go of a dead situation.

Isn't it amazing, how we try to delay the inevitable? This is especially true for relationships. But when it's dead and gone, let it go. Be you the initiator, or the one being expelled, breaking up is never an easy thing to do. But to begin, we'll deal with the situation from the side of the initiator. By the time you declare, 'It's over,' typically your only regret is that you didn't live up to the statement sooner.

At the inception of any relationship, not a single one of us starts out thinking, 'this love affair isn't going to work,' let alone be the source of so much wasted time, misery, or heartache. Adding insult to injury, someone probably told you, 'You're making a huge mistake' or 'This is cool, but it's not the right person.' Now in hindsight, you can't help but see it. Moreover, the person who said that, more than likely, was you. At any rate, when something is over, it's over.

When the relationship began, chances are you were ensnared by the idea of 'romance.' Perhaps you weren't thinking straight but that's not the case anymore. Regrettably, you chose not to listen to your voice of reason. Now that you have started the process of moving on with your life, let's finish that old relationship once and for all. Stop looking back. You can't get to your destination if you're going to drive while staring in the rear view mirror. Not only is that counter productive, it could kill you. Truth is, you are delaying your real blessing.

Naturally, it was not your intent to fail at this last attempt at romance; however, you stumbled headlong into this situation without taking the time to analyze your circumstances. Like many of us, you probably fell into this relationship based on convenience, proximity or loneliness. During such moments, it's easy to be bewitched by the fruits of what was perceived to be the rewards from a love tree. Herein lies the problem. If you stand too close to the tree you don't see the dangers of the forest. Compare this to standing too close to a mirror—you can see yourself, but your face fills the frame so you can't focus on understanding the whole picture.

How can you make a good decision without considering all the facts? Knowledge is power and people perish for a lack of it. They 'fall in love' thoughtlessly. But, think about it, is falling into something ever safe? Of course not. Falling into something even sounds unwise, let alone is it prudent. To make a good decision you must consider all the facts.

How can you serve two masters without betraying one for the other? That is, you can't be in and out of a dysfunctional relationship. If you are going to find the joy that God wants for you, then you must permanently release the bad relationship.

Feelings change. One moment you can be happy, the next sad. Sometimes you're fed up, the next you're glad. That is why you stayed on this hellish merry-go-round so long or became involved in a relationship because the person seemed nice during a time of stress. You allowed feelings instead of wisdom to direct you.

Love is not a situation or an emotion. It's a state of

being, a decision, a habitat. The good part about the human condition is that we're always prone to want love. The bad part is that we confuse 'love' with feelings and in many instances we desire it under any condition and that's true even if it's packaged in something that our gut instincts and common sense tell us to avoid—whether it's an abusive situation, a married man or woman, unequally balanced lifestyles, a familiar friend or other inappropriate partnering.

It is my opinion, that's why most people remain in dying or dysfunctional relationships. Chasing feelings, people catapult themselves back and forth into what they believe is love, only to wind up worse off than last time. Ninety percent of the time, feelings are guided by ego, pride, familiarity and lust. Sometimes it's good to pray and think before you act. But faith without works is dead so asking God to help you through this is one thing; doing your part is another. Let Him and your spirit guide you, but pay attention to the process and do your share of the work.

Prayer changes things, provided that you listen after you pray. Let's take the time to examine what that really means.

- You will have to do your homework.
- Work is seldom fun.
- It needs to be done when you least feel like doing it.
- Seldom will you like the work.
- But you will always love the results.

We're going to use this as a premise because a map is not good unless it is used. Finding your path to a quality relationship requires thought. When we were children, our parents told us, 'Walk, don't run—you may get hurt.' 'Look, before you leap—you may dive into an empty pool.' 'Think, before you speak—you can't take back words.' 'Think before you act—you can't un-strike a match.' Do we listen? Of course not! That's because were acting on impulse, emotion and feelings without considering the impact of an incompetent decision-making process.

Just because something looks, smells, tastes or makes you feel good, doesn't mean that it's good for you. Examine nature and you'll note that the most attractive animals and plants are often the most dangerous. By no means am I suggesting that because someone is attractive, or a situation is appealing, that it's inherently bad. That's far from the truth. What I'm suggesting is, what you feel is beautiful can in reality be a very ugly thing so look for the beauty but engage your mind and be attentive to the big picture surrounding it. Remember, it's better to do things right instead of fast. Just because it feels good for the moment doesn't mean you should do it.

I'm sure before you began this last relationship your inner voice urged you to be a bit more patient, chill, or run like hell, but you didn't heed it. Your feelings overshadowed your common sense. I'm going to provide a mental map that will help you distinguish your Spirit from your mind, and your feelings. Find a pen and paper, then write this down:

Horse = Feelings = Id

Man = Mind = Ego

Spirit = Bridle = Super Ego

Picture a man riding a horse. The horse is the Id. It follows instinct, reacts to the environment, has no sense of direction, and is guided by raw feelings. The man controls the horse; if he doesn't, the horse will go where it wants, when it wants. Making matters worse, the horse is trying to control him but if the man stays in control and disciplined, he maintains command over the horse and reaches his destination every time. The Spirit is what has been given to the man to empower him to navigate his way through life. It also assists in controlling the horse. He doesn't have to use it, but the more he does, the easier the horse will be to control.

You should see that you are already equipped for the journey called your life. However, if you are going to manifest your destiny you must understand how to listen to your spirit and control your horse. A huge piece to that puzzle is paying attention to the signs that God gives you, better known as 'red flags.'

God uses people, places and things to communicate the answers to your prayers. Don't be surprised when He uses your intuition or your instincts. Next time that little voice tells you, 'You're moving too fast' you may want to do more than hear it, try listening. 'Listening' by definition is taking notice of, and acting on, what you hear. Just as my dad knew something I didn't know, your inner being knows what you don't. Especially when your instinct tells you: 'Don't rush into this,' 'This isn't a good idea,' 'That didn't sound right,' or 'Run like hell!'

Red flags are there for a reason. Even a broken watch is right twice a day, but do not set a schedule by it. As a young man, my father constantly told me, 'Slow down son, you're moving a little too fast.' Similar to many of you, instead of listening to the voice of reason, I did the exact opposite. Immature people don't value common sense. My thought process was, 'I'm a grown man, I know what I'm doing.'

Hint: Age doesn't make you mature, wisdom does.

The first step in growth is learning that all actions come with consequences. As a younger man, I was guided by emotions, pride and negative ego, not wisdom. Allowing those forces to shepherd me cost me a great deal in wasted time and lost opportunities—time and chances that none of us can get back.

People confuse intelligence with common sense. Or, at times we presume we know everything but nothing can be further from the truth. The Bible says, 'A wise man heeds the counsel of good advisors bearing fruit.' Isn't it time that we learn from our mistakes? Only a fool keeps doing the same thing over and over, expecting a different outcome.

Some of life's lessons are learned by making mistakes. There is an old saying: 'Three ways to learn something: If you have to use your hands, you learn by doing. If you're wise, you learn by listening. If you're a damn fool, you learn by not listening.' Often, we go through unnecessary heartache and suffering because we simply don't listen. I knew what wisdom was, but I was caught up in my world and too immature to consider that I could be wrong. My advice to you is, don't do that! Too many times we have blinders on and don't value listening to the voice of reason.

More often than not, we suffer needless losses from irrational judgement. Making matters worse, what you forsake can't easily be replaced, if at all. You can give it your best shot, but seldom can you substitute something new or functioning in place of what God was trying to give. What's most tragic is that the mess you're going through could have easily been avoided. The lesson here is to trust God.

The Word says, 'When I was a child, I thought as a child. Now that I'm a man, it's time to put away childish things.' With experience comes wisdom. Failing to heed the voice of reason comes with a hefty price tag: loss. There's a reason we lose valuable things in life—not thinking. Many such losses result from failing to realize the significance of the things that really matter. In many instances, by the time we do, it's too little, too late.

Most relationship problems possess the potential to be resolved; however, if you wait too long and do not correct mistakes in a timely manner, more than likely you won't be successful. Lost, wasted, destroyed, or misused opportunities result in regret, emptiness and turmoil. Here are a few examples of things that 'I'm sorry,' 'I should have,' 'I could have,' 'I meant to,' and money can't fix:

- ◆ You can't replace a broken heart.
- ◆ You can't regain trust.
- ◆ You can't replace wasted youth.
- ◆ You can't replace innocence.
- ◆ You can't replace time.
- ◆ You can't replace opportunity.
- ◆ You can't replace pivotal moments.

How many times have you attempted to recapture stolen moments and lost hope, only to realize it was too little, too late? If you haven't learned anything else from this breakup, you should be learning that life and time are two things you cannot afford to waste. That's why you must maximize this moment!

On many occasions my father attempted to stop me from making rash, spontaneous decisions, but my first thought was he didn't know what he was talking about. I remember thinking, 'This is my life, he's not standing in my shoes, how could he conceivably understand where I'm coming from?' As he was speaking to me, I'd look at him with indifference, not appreciating his insight (usually due to the fact it went against what I wanted to do). In comparison, I am sure your instinct uttered the same simple phrase to you: 'Something isn't right here, slow your roll, stop.' Isn't it amazing how we can so easily get a case of functional deafness? Ignoring sound judgement or your inner voice will cost you every time.

I promise you that every bad 'love' decision you ever

made was preceded by a warning sign that you ignored. Ninety percent of the time a number of cues along the way indicate that you should stop and look before you go any further. Your instincts are constantly advising you that this may not be a wise decision.

Signs are tools. By definition, a 'sign' is an object, quality, or event, whose presence or occurrence indicates the probable presence or occurrence of something else. Signs are instruments that God uses to indicate something is taking place that you need not ignore. Life's omens should be regarded as a warning or evidence that something is happening or going to happen. Not paying attention to the signs that a relationship is bad for you early in the game can be detrimental.

Something as simple as a traffic sign or a signal light is put in place to prevent us from experiencing unnecessary harm. A sign in your life benefits you when its purpose is fully understood. That's why we need to examine why God puts the signs in our lives. Back to our example: A stop sign is placed at an intersection for a reason: To avoid the negative consequences of collisions, injuries, or needless deaths. Nobody simply placed a sign there because they were bored. The same thing is true for the signs surrounding the circumstances involving your relationship. God allows us to see signs that warn you that things aren't right. It's up to you to heed them.

Here is another tip: It's never the big things that God uses to get our attention. It's the subtle things. I strongly recommend that you examine what signs are present before, not after, you start your next relationship. Before you go overboard and turn into a sleuth, I'm suggesting that you examine both your own and your potential mate's motives. Prior to attempting a relationship with anyone, consider the aspects that are vital to success. Confirm that you have common goals, shared spiritual beliefs and possess similar aspirations. For a relationship to work, you must be equally yoked. Although people typically associate that with finances, the concept behind being equally yoked goes much deeper than that. I refer to characteristics such as social values, principles, lifestyle, and shared interests. Like morals and ethics are essential.

I'm willing to bet, as you and your ex talked, significant differences of opinion surfaced but the subject was either avoided, changed or ignored. Throwing trash in the closet does not tidy the room; you just get a messy closet. That's the equivalent of having your dog leave a souvenir in your bedroom and you just kicking it under the bed.

Neither does the ostrich principle work in relationships. Let me provide an illustration of the ostrich principle. Please picture this: A pride of lions is stalking the Serengeti and, as they proceed, the ostrich notices them from a distance. Instead of that fool running away while he's got the chance, the ostrich feels stress so he finds a hole and sticks his head in it. Granted, he can't see the lions anymore. But, does that make his problem go away? Of course not! The same is true for you. Just because you put yourself in a position not to see your problem doesn't mean it's not there anymore.

THE FIRST STEP IN HEALING

I stated earlier that only a fool continues to do the same thing over and over and expect a different outcome. The first step of your healing process is to comprehend why this last relationship failed. If you don't examine that carefully, I can guarantee that you will make the same mistake again and again. The only thing that will change is the date on the calendar and the names of the people. The only way to avoid future problems is to analyze the source of your previous predicaments. Avoiding serious conversations is not a solution either; if anything, it is the spawning ground for a series of setbacks and obstacles down the road. Not dealing with serious issues was a catalyst for this breakup.

Unfortunately, we focus too easily on what we want, what makes us feel good or what gives us temporary happiness. Good looks, money, great sex, and lots of fun are the fruits of a good relationship. However, not one of these ingredients is the source of one. I doubt seriously if you began your last relationship planning to fail. Be honest with yourself—the truth is you failed to plan.

If you are going to develop a successful relationship one must construct a firm foundation; pandemonium results without it. Then, what could have been a really good relationship results in commotion, confusion, turmoil, and disarray, ending in failure.

Everything in a relationship has a price tag. Another way to look at breaking up is comparing managing love to managing money. To maintain a healthy financial picture you must plan, monitor and practice sound administration of resources. Failing to do this with money or a relationship results in the same outcome, disaster. If you don't manage your finances you are destined to reach a state of misery. Emotional tragedy results in mental and emotional ruin. As mental or financial resources are exhausted, you're left with an unfavorable but necessary solution, bankruptcy.

Bankruptcy is likened to the breakup stage of a relationship. It is a very unpleasant thing but the up side is that it's a new beginning. The same thing is true about a breakup. Breaking up does not mean breaking down. Like bankruptcy, it gives you the opportunity to start anew. It allows you to understand how important it is to properly plan and manage your emotional and mental resources. Before you start another relationship you must understand the importance of evaluating yourself, the other person and the potential effect you have on one another. Not doing so is equal to spending money out of a checking account and not writing down the balance after each expenditure. You will be broke, in this case broken, before you know what hit you.

This time before you run out and find another new lover, let's get to know you. Not the you that you have become, not the you whom others say you are, but get acquainted with the real you, the person God created you to be. The process of self-actualization is a necessary endeavor. How can you succeed in understanding anyone else if you don't fully understand yourself? Self-actualization is simply defined as understanding and knowing yourself for whom and what you really are. If you are facing insolvency, you don't just walk away from your debts. The bankruptcy court requires that you be accountable for the situation and wants you to demonstrate a plan to get yourself out. The same thing is true for ending your relationship and starting anew.

MAKE A PERSONAL ACCOUNTING

The judiciary of life demands that you take a good look at what created your current situation. Now is the season to assess what and how things happened, what went wrong, what is it you could have and should have done. This time requires that you take a serious look at you and your ex. This process is an autopsy not a reunion. Examine why both of you are the way you are. Evaluate yourself and the person that you broke up with. Write down your flaws and theirs. This is a time to be very truthful with yourself.

Don't use this exercise as a walk down memory lane; nor is it a weapon to indict yourself, your former mate, or stock your war chests. The purpose of this exercise is to inoculate yourself in order to avoid making the same mistakes in the future. This process is intended to facilitate change and catalyze maturity. List some of the things that your ex said about you and the things you said about them. Examine the cause-and-effect relationship between situations and circumstances that facilitated these accusations. This is not a quest for justification or excuses but another tool that we are using to empower you and stop you from repeating the same mistakes again. Take the time to do some critical thinking.

On a separate sheet of paper, write down what would have happened had you or your ex done things differently. Use your hypothetical findings to define the new you. If you want transformation in your life, you cannot go backwards. Compel yourself to leave the past behind and redefine yourself for the future. Every successful business does an audit at least four times a year. Only by examining accounts do you know where you stand. The most important business you have is your life. Audit it. Once you know where you are, then you possess the facts you need to in order to get where you're going. Only a fool begins a journey without first assessing the cost.

God may have allowed you to get in this situation, but it was your doing, not his. Now allow Him to get you out. Last, but not least, now that the pharaoh's dead, you're free to leave Egypt.

CHAPTER 2

WHAT GOD HAS JOINED

FRIENDS, FAMILY, AND RELIGIOUS ISSUES

Coping with a breakup is never easy, and coming to grips with your frustration and anger can be stressful until all the issues are resolved. Plus, dealing with guilt and confronting the opinions of relatives, in-laws, and your circle of friends can be a major source of irritation. It's bad enough to live up to the way someone else thinks you're supposed to live, but when you abandon yourself to fulfill their illusion, you are headed for serious trouble.

Besides that, several other factors are involved in this

dilemma. These range from dealing with karma, coming to terms with a relationship that was based on everything but the right thing, and being embittered due to broken promises. Most often the worst of these is the guilt associated with religious beliefs and keeping up appearances. Here are a few facts and statistics on divorce. For those of you who aren't married, keep reading; this applies to you too!

In 2009 the United States Center for Disease Control quoted the following statistics on marriage and divorce:

Number of marriages in 2008: 2,162,000

Marriage rate: 7.1 per 1,000 total population

Divorce rate: 3.5 per 1,000 population (44 reporting states and D.C.)[1]

In simple terms, over two million people got married in the year 2008. For every 1000 Americans, there were 7.1 marriages, out of 44 reporting states and the District of Columbia; 3.5 of those marriages ended in divorce. In other words, for every seven couples that married, there were 3.5 divorces. Over fifty percent of marriages in the United States failed last year. For every two marriages there was at least one completed divorce. Not included are those that separated, filed for divorce and haven't yet completed the process yet, or the people that left to go to the store and have yet to return.

---

[1] Births, Marriages, Divorces, and Deaths: Provisional Data for 2008, Table A

After speaking with hundreds of people, my findings indicate the hardest part of a breakup or divorce is not the breakup itself, it's issues dealing with the guilt trip. Often, the problem is coming to terms with one's own religious views on divorce. Second to that is dealing with the opinions of relatives, friends, church members and social groups. But remember, your family members will have opinions no matter what you do. Third, the most recurrent problem is keeping the status quo or maintaining appearances. But I want you to set out by telling yourself, 'Don't play with love.' God is Love and He doesn't play. Love does not harm, it heals. With that stated, we'll continue.

RELIGION AND DIVORCE

Let's start by examining some common religious views on divorce and breaking up. In many religions divorce is not considered an acceptable outcome to a divine arrangement. Since I am most familiar with the Christian religion, I'll use that as my example. A Christian wedding typically begins with this phrase, 'In the presence of Almighty God, we are gathered here today to join this couple in holy matrimony.' The end of the ceremony states, 'What God has joined let no man put asunder.' Before you start having a guilt trip, keep reading. God allows for mistakes! I'll continue with my example of Christianity and its views on divorce.

It's no wonder that people feel such guilt when their marriage does not work. Most people are getting second-hand information and not reading or researching the word 'divorce' for themselves. Before starting your crucifixion or reopening the Spanish Inquisition, let's examine what the Bible actually says concerning divorce. I'm going to quote some passages that will comfort you. In the 19 chapter of Matthew, Jesus said it's okay to get a divorce if there is sexual immorality. Deuteronomy 24 states that indecency provides grounds for divorce. Second Corinthians, the sixth chapter, says don't be unequally yoked with unbelievers.

Although I am not an expert on Islamic, Hindu nor Buddhist religions, I will be daring enough to suggest that the theological views of God are the same across the religious spectrum: God is a God of Love and He is just. He is the author of all faiths and all spirituality, Man is the founder of doctrinarism and religion. I suggest you fear God not man. I suggest that you avoid listening to some sexist clergyman with a hidden agenda; study the Holy Word on your own, whatever your belief system.

The following is based on my Internet research.

Islam and divorce: The Qur'an talks about the grounds for divorce in very general terms: 'And if you fear that the two (i.e. husband and wife) may not be able to keep the limits ordered by Allah, there is no blame on either of them if she redeems herself (from the marriage tie)' (2:229).

The general grounds for divorce in the Qur'an, therefore, is hopeless failure of one or both parties to discharge their marital duties and to consort with each other in kindness, peace and compassion. The jurists have developed some indices, which may be accepted as grounds of divorce in case the divorce matter goes to the court. Long absence of husband without any information, long imprisonment, refusal to provide for wife, impotence etc. are some of the grounds on which wife can ask for divorce. Either party may take steps to divorce in case of disease, insanity, deceptive misrepresentation during marriage contract, desertion etc.

A Muslim male is allowed three chances, that is to say, three pronouncements or acts of divorce on three different occasions provided that each divorce is pronounced during the time when the wife is in the period of parity (that is not in her menstrual time). A husband may divorce his wife once and let the Iddat (the period of waiting after divorce) pass. During the waiting period the two have the option of being reconciled. If, however, the waiting period passes without reconciliation, they stand fully divorced.

If after the first divorce the husband is reconciled with his wife but the hostility and conflict begins all over again, he may divorce her a second time in the same manner as stated above. In this case, also, he can return to her during the Iddat (or waiting period.) If, however, after second reconciliation, he divorces the wife the third time, he can not take back the wife during the Iddat. She is totally prohibited for him. The lady, thereafter, can marry any person she likes according to her choice.[2]

---

[2] Yusuf al-Qaradawi, 'The Lawful and Prohibited in Islam,' at www.witness-pioneer.org/ vil/Books/Q_LP/index.htm

Hinduism and divorce: In ancient times, women in Hindu society had limited freedom. Nothing like the modern concept of divorce existed in Hindu society. Once a woman left her parents, she was completely at the mercy of her husband and, if her husband found her incompatible or unattractive and abandoned her, there was little that she could do. She had no right to divorce and no right to remarry, nor did she have the right to leave the house and approach anyone without her husband's permission. In case of men the situation is totally different. Men have many rights and privileges, which they exercised in the name of religion, family or expediency.

According to the Hindu marriage act of 1955 (India), divorce is possible on certain grounds: adultery, cruelty, desertion for two years, religious conversion, mental abnormality, venereal disease, leprosy, renunciation of the world, physical separation, absence of communication for more than seven years. A woman can also seek divorce from her husband if he is guilty of rape, sodomy or bestiality. According to the Hindu marriage act, a dependent spouse (male or female) can petition the court for alimony. About custody of children there is no clear-cut law. Courts have to decide the matter on the individual merits of each case.[3]

Buddhism and divorce: Divorce, although uncommon for Buddhists, is not prohibited. It is expected, however, that if a couple enters into marriage and adheres to

---

[3] Jarayam V, 'Divorce in Hinduism,' at www.hinduwebsite.com/ hinduism/h_divorce.asp

Buddhism's ethical prescriptions for marital and family life, that divorce becomes a non-issue. If, however, a couple refuses to follow the ethical prescriptions, is unable to live in peace, harmony, and mutuality with one another, or extreme circumstances, such as adultery or violence exist, it is preferable for the marriage to be broken rather than for the marriage to destroy the couple or the family.[4]

It is not my goal to begin some religious debate on marriage and divorce; however, I do intend to make some very simple points. These rules apply to you even if you weren't legally married. God, no matter how you refer to Him, did not create marriage or relationships for anyone to be abused, mistreated, taken for granted, and made miserable. Marriage is designed to be productive, fruitful and to multiply the human race. You cannot be productive if you are stressed, depressed, mistreated, frustrated, living a lie, or abused. How can you be fruitful if you're stifled? Who in their right mind wants to replicate or multiply problems?

Don't let anyone use religion to take advantage of your good nature. This is especially true for those of us who subscribe to a higher calling, faith in God or a reverent belief system. Historically women have been unfairly judged and mistreated by all religions. I am in no way suggesting that all male religious leaders practice sexism; many honorable and decent men can be found in all

---

[4] F. Matthew Schobert, Jr., and Scott. W. Taylor, 'Buddhism and the Family,' at family.jrank.org/pages/183/Buddhism-Buddhism-Family.html#ixzz0aXosaAR7

religions. However, my research finds that in the Old Testament of the Christian Bible there are many sexist presentations concerning the subject of divorce and women. Unfortunately, many similar attitudes exist in almost all other religions. Ladies and gentlemen, please remember, God is not a bigot, racist or sexist. He intended for all of us to be treated with love, decency, and respect.

Every holy book that I have read has a common theme: We are to love our neighbors as we love ourselves. So how can we love God, whom we cannot see, and mistreat those that we can? A man or woman should love their mate as much as they love themselves. The Word also tells us, 'Do not cast your pearls before swine' and 'Be wise as a serpent and harmless as a dove.' The Christian Bible states, 'In as much as you've done to the least of these, you have also done to me (i.e., God).' God is telling you, don't be a fool for anybody. That includes husbands, wives, significant others, fiancées, boy and girl friends, and, especially, yourself.

Marriage is the supreme commitment; nonetheless, if there are children, blended families, shared finances, and years of a relationship involved, what's right is right. Just because you are not legally married, you're not excused. These rules apply to significant others, fiancées, even boyfriends and girlfriends. Not only is it wrong for someone to use your relationship with God, faith, or creed as a manipulation tool or blackmail device to keep you in a dysfunctional relationship, it's trifling. There is a big difference between legacy and tradition. Just because your mom or dad put up with being ill-treated does not mean that you should. If they jumped in a trash compactor, would you? Legacy is one thing, but tradition is another.

A legacy is a set of standards that upholds honor, character, virtue, principles and morals. Legacies protect and enhance the meaning, and create value in life. Tradition, on the other hand, is quite the opposite; it often takes aim at, and often takes advantage of, those things. Traditions can be either bad or good. It depends on what they are and how they affect the lives of the people affected by them.

A good tradition like jumping a broom or kissing under mistletoe is one thing, but practices based on institutionalism or habit can be chancy at best or even perilous. Some traditions, like gender bias, sexism, racism, abuse and disloyalty have been the downfall of relationships. The worst of all traditions is stupidity and ignorance. The term 'stupid' implies a sluggish, slow-witted lack of intelligence. This is brought on by people accepting the status quo, settling for less than they deserve, and accepting mediocrity as a standard. Stupidity, like genetics, is often passed down. Ignorance is simply a lack of knowledge, but after reading this you cannot use that as an excuse any more.

Here is an example of both stupidity and tradition:

Three sisters gathered at their grandmother's house on Thanksgiving Day to prepare the holiday meal. As the family sat in the den a commotion arose in the kitchen.

The sisters were arguing about how to prepare and cut the holiday ham. Grandmother had always cut it prior to putting it into the oven. Now one sister said, 'It should be cut in the center.' Another sister said, 'Cut it by the shank.' And the oldest sister said, 'Cut it on the far end.' After a couple of hours of arguing and bickering, Grandmother came in the kitchen and asked, 'Why in the devil are you three cussing so loud? What are you arguing about?' All of them stated their points vehemently. Then their Grandmother spit her teeth out laughing. At that moment their mother walked in and asked, 'What in the Hell is going on in here?' After hearing the story she looked at her Mother and said, 'Momma do you want to tell them or should I?' Grandmother said, 'You tell those three fools why I would cut the ham.' The girls' mother laughed for about five minutes then told them the truth behind the tradition. She said, 'Mom cut the ham because her stove was too little for the whole ham to fit in it.'

Sometimes, when you uncover why you're following a tradition, you look like a fool for doing so. Some people remain in bad relationships because they saw Mom or Dad put up with being abused, cheated on, or mistreated. Tradition is not always a good thing, but using common sense is.

Many people remain in dysfunctional relationships due to the influence of relatives, church members, friends and poor role models. My advice is to tell those obtuse people to 'go to hell' (though please don't say that literally!) and stay out your business. I realize that sounds cruel, but you might as well tell them to go there, especially since that's where they're insisting you reside!

It is not reasonable that you be made to suffer at the hands of someone who is deceptive, abusive and manipulative. Furthermore, it is equally unjust for you to have someone use guilt as a tool to bind you or someone else to a malfunctioning situation. Both men and women are victims of a congregational or collective mindset. Just because someone else says it's right doesn't make it so. You have the right to be happy and so does your former mate.

Being equally yoked is crucial to the success of a relationship. A house divided will never stand. How can two people be successful at anything unless they both agree? Though many people emphasize finances when they consider being equally yoked, it takes much more than money to be happy. As a matter of fact, I have seen many poor couples stand the test of time; whereas, I have seen many wealthy families disintegrate when the least amount of pressure is applied. Consider the example of two horses pulling a carriage. If one is going north and the other headed south you're not going to get anywhere. Strong relationships are based on a commitment to excellence. Without dedication, devotion, allegiance, loyalty, faithfulness, and fidelity the chance of failure is great.

KEY INGREDIENTS IN RELATIONSHIPS

Now that we are headed in the right direction, let's use the mistakes of the past to ensure your future. For a relationship to work you will need some key ingredients.

The first is a commitment to integrity. Without trust, you have no relationship. Ability to count on your mate is key, but that's just half of the equation. You have a part to play too. Your mate needs to be able to believe in, and count on, you too. A relationship without dependability will possess no stability. Disclosure is everything. There is no point in hiding the truth because it's going to tell on you sooner rather than later. I have counseled many couples who were trying to repair lost trust. It's easier to glue scales back on a wet fish.

Another key ingredient is dedication. By definition, 'dedication' means being committed to the task or a purpose. There is a difference between knowing when to walk away versus cracking under pressure. Walk away when your tomorrows are rooted in useless, detrimental, destructive, and hurtful yesterdays. Allegiance is necessary to maintain loyalty but if goals are to be achieved, sooner or later, both parties will eventually take subordinate roles in the relationship. Take pledging allegiance to the flag. This proclamation demonstrates our public devotion and instills personal dedication to the purpose of democracy. But it does no good if you don't believe what you're saying and merely repeat the pledge out of habit, not commitment. A promise means nothing if you can't keep it.

Next, but certainly not least, is faithfulness and fidelity. Faithfulness is the act of being steadfast and constant. Earlier I stated that love is a condition. What good is a condition, if it is unstable? It's no good at all. Would you drive a car if the brakes didn't work consistently? Of course not. You feel secure when what you trust in is reliable. Fidelity can only be demonstrated by continuing loyalty and support. Favorable outcomes are the result of intention not coincidence. If you can't be trusted or cannot trust your mate, it is a waste of time.

The next ingredient is building on a solid foundation. In the previous chapter, I mentioned that people don't plan to fail, they fail to plan. Nothing is more true. A key factor in planning is beginning with the right ingredients. Your past relationship failed because of substandard ingredients. There are some things that you cannot substitute, including common sense and honesty. Relationships that are birthed out of deception, manipulation, money, convenience or adultery never work. You will reap what you sow and if you put garbage in you will get garbage out. Plant the seeds of truth, integrity, right-mindedness, positive statements, supportive actions, and compassionate attitudes if you to reap success.

If you're to embrace your future you must release the past. That means you can't hold on to old lovers, ex in-laws, and old habits in order to make a new and stronger connection. Imagine that you're attending a circus, you see the men on the trapeze. Typically one will swing in order to build momentum to reach the other. When enough energy is built up, the two men establish a matched rhythm. The harmony strengthens them to move toward the same place at the same time. As one follows the other's lead, their timing becomes synchronized. Do you recall that earlier I said you must work together if you are to achieve any goal?

Success is the result of making a very strong, purposely coordinated connection Because they're in sync, the trapeze artists end up at the same place at the same time. Rapport, oneness and coordination enable them to reach out and touch one another. This is the point where one grabs the other, and together they reach the other side safely and successfully. Despite the turns, flips, and theatrics, great timing is the key to a successful conclusion.

What good is all that effort be if one or the other does not release their respective bars? Ask yourself: Why have I built up all this momentum to get to the other side and am afraid to move forward? What is it that I'm hanging onto? Is hanging on to my past going to help or interfere with my goals? More than likely you and your partner will wind up stuck hanging in the middle of nowhere. Remember: Remaining in a defective relationship makes at least four people miserable. You, the person you're with and the two people that God intended you to be with.

ESTABLISHING YOUR NEW IDENTITY

Embracing the new you will require getting into some new social circles and establishing your own identity. If you're going to move forward, it is imperative that you let go of everything that's connected to your past. Unfortunately, this includes letting go of your ex's family (yes, I did say that earlier, but some of you need to hear that again.) That means releasing some of your and your old lover's mutual friends.

Addicts, alcoholics and people with dependent personalities do not function well, if at all, until they lose contact with the source of the problem. This is especially true when it relates to those who are in negative, addictive, abusive relationships. It's not realistic to expect change for your life when you don't allow change in your life.

Just as people use drugs as a crutch, people caught in dysfunctional relationships tend to hang on to ex-spouses, fiancés, and significant others friends and relatives. Believe it or not, often this is done for selfish and manipulative reasons. Ask yourself this question: Are you cleaving to your ex's relatives and friends? If children are involved that's one thing, but if not, you're hindering your growth. If this is a behavior that you continue to demonstrate, check yourself or get counseling. Remember, there is nothing wrong with getting help if deeper issues are present. Otherwise, just ask yourself what your motive is if you're doing this. You may be doing it to rub salt in the face of an ex or simply to be nosey. I strongly suggest that you Google, 'Let it go by TD Jakes.' Stop tripping and know that God is not through with you yet.

The last factor in this stage of breaking up is ridding yourself of the concern over how you think other people perceive you. What is more important: how you're doing or how it appears you're doing? How you're doing is far more crucial than how it appears you're doing.

Question: Are you being so many things to so many people that you don't know whom you are anymore? When is the last time you have been true to yourself, let alone someone else? It's time to take responsibility for your actions, stop blaming everything and everybody. You're responsible for what you have allowed in your life.

Not long ago I was watching CNN and heard the following story.

A prominent female lawyer talk show host was discussing relationships gone bad. After several moments of male bashing, she asked one of her guests, who happened to be a female lawyer and author, 'Are you angry about your divorce?' Her reply was, 'No.' Then she continued to ask who was at fault for the divorce. Much to my surprise the guest made the following comments. 'I had bad vibes about the marriage to start with. Something told me not to go through with it. But I decided to do so because we had invited all these guests. The church was reserved, I bought a wedding dress and had a formal announcement put in the paper, not to mention all the gifts we received. After years of living a lie, I realized that the whole thing was a mistake.' This particular guest happened to be a very famous legal expert and author. My reason for sharing that story is to point out that wealth, fame and fortune don't stop people from making dumb mistakes.

Before you and I judge this woman, I have a confession to make. The exact same thing happened to me. Not taking anything away from my ex-wife. She gave me four wonderful children that I love dearly. Not to mention that she is a very sweet person (happily remarried) and we are very good friends—now. But, I caused her, myself and innocent children unnecessary pain and heartache because I wasn't man enough to do the right thing. Thank God for grace, my kids are now well-rounded young adults. Nonetheless, my not speaking up put all of us through needless heartache, pain and stress. Just like the sister on CNN, I was more concerned about how things appeared than how they were. The way things are is far more important than how they look.

A parable is often a far better teaching tool than any set of instructions. At the conclusion of this chapter I am going to share a story written by Hans Christian Andersen titled, 'The Emperor's New Clothes.' Though this was written over three hundred years ago, isn't it funny that the truth never changes. Many of us are so surrounded by people who are living a lie themselves that, before we know it, we start living one too.

'The Emperor's New Clothes'
by Hans Christian Andersen (1805-75)[5]

Many years ago there lived an Emperor who was so exceedingly fond of fine new clothes that he spent vast sums of money on dress. To him clothes meant more than anything else in the world. Everyone knew about the

---

[5] Adapted by Sara and Stephen Corrin in *Stories for Seven-Year-Olds*, Faber and Faber, 1964

Emperor's passion for clothes.

Now one fine day two swindlers, calling themselves weavers, arrived. They declared that they could make the most magnificent cloth that one could imagine; cloth of most beautiful colours and elaborate patterns. Not only was the material so beautiful, but the clothes made from it had the special power of being invisible to everyone who was stupid or not fit for his post.

So the Emperor gave the swindlers large sums of money and the two weavers set up their looms in the palace. They demanded the finest thread of the best silk and the finest gold and they pretended to work at their looms. But they put nothing on the looms. The frames stood empty. The silk and gold thread they stuffed into their bags. So they sat pretending to weave, and continued to work at the empty loom till late into the night. Night after night they went home with their money and their bags full of the finest silk and gold thread. Day after day they pretended to work.

Now the Emperor was eager to know how much of the cloth was finished, and would have loved to see for himself. He was, however, somewhat uneasy. 'Suppose,' he thought secretly, 'suppose I am unable to see the cloth. That would mean I am either stupid or unfit for my post. That cannot be,' he thought, but all the same he decided to send for his faithful old minister to go and see. 'He will best be able to see how the cloth looks. He is far from stupid and splendid at his work.'

The Emperor's minister opened his eyes wide. 'Upon

my life!' he thought. 'I see nothing at all, nothing.' But he did not say so.

The two swindlers begged him to come nearer and asked him how he liked it. 'Are not the colors exquisite, and see how intricate are the patterns,' they said. The poor old minister stared and stared. Still he could see nothing, for there was nothing. But he did not dare to say he saw nothing. 'Nobody must find out," thought he. 'I must never confess that I could not see the stuff.'

'Well,' said one of the rascals. 'You do not say whether it pleases you.'

'Oh, it is beautiful—most excellent, to be sure. Such a beautiful design, such exquisite colors. I shall tell the Emperor how enchanted I am with the cloth.'

'We are very glad to hear that,' said the weavers, and they started to describe the colors and patterns in great detail. The old minister listened very carefully so that he could repeat the description to the Emperor. They also demanded more money and more gold thread, saying that they needed it to finish the cloth. But, of course, they put all they were given into their bags and pockets and kept on working at their empty looms.

Soon after this the Emperor sent another official to see how the men were getting on and to ask whether the cloth would soon be ready. Exactly the same happened with him as with the minister. He stood and stared, but as there was nothing to be seen, he could see nothing.

'Is not the material beautiful?' said the swindlers, and

again they talked of 'the patterns and the exquisite colors. 'Stupid I certainly am not,' thought the official. 'Then I must be unfit for my post. But nobody shall know that I could not see the material.' Then he praised the material he did not see and declared that he was delighted with the colors and the marvelous patterns.

To the Emperor he said when he returned, 'The cloth the weavers are preparing is truly magnificent.'

And now the Emperor was curious to see the costly stuff for himself while it was still upon the looms. Accompanied by a number of selected ministers, among whom were the two poor ministers who had already been before, the Emperor went to the weavers. There they sat in front of the empty looms, weaving more diligently than ever, yet without a single thread upon the looms.

'Is not the cloth magnificent?' said the two ministers. 'See here, the splendid pattern, the glorious colors.' Each pointed to the empty loom. Each thought that the other could see the material.

'What can this mean?' said the Emperor to himself. 'This is terrible. Am I so stupid? Am I not fit to be Emperor? This is disastrous,' he thought. But aloud he said, 'Oh, the cloth is perfectly wonderful. It has a splendid pattern and such charming colors.' And he nodded his approval and smiled appreciatively and stared at the empty looms. He would not, he could not, admit he saw nothing, when his two ministers had praised the material so highly. And all his men looked and looked at the empty looms.

Not one of them saw anything there at all. Nevertheless, they all said, 'Oh, the cloth is magnificent.'

The rascals sat up all that night and worked, burning more than sixteen candles, so that everyone could see how busy they were making the suit of clothes ready for the procession. Each of them had a great big pair of scissors and they cut in the air, pretending to cut the cloth with them, and sewed with needles without any thread.

There was great excitement in the palace and the Emperor's clothes were the talk of the town. At last the weavers declared that the clothes were ready. Then the Emperor, with the most distinguished gentlemen of the court, came to the weavers. Each of the swindlers lifted up an arm as if he were holding something. 'Here are Your Majesty's trousers,' said one. 'This is Your Majesty's mantle,' said the other. 'The whole suit is as light as a spider's web. Why, you might almost feel as if you had nothing on, but that is just the beauty of it.'

'Magnificent,' cried the ministers, but they could see nothing at all. Indeed there was nothing to be seen.

'Now if Your Imperial Majesty would graciously consent to take off your clothes,' said the weavers, 'we could fit on the new ones.' So the Emperor laid aside his clothes and the swindlers pretended to help him into the new ones they were supposed to have made.

The Emperor turned from side to side in front of the long glass as if admiring himself.

'How well they fit. How splendid Your Majesty's robes

look: What gorgeous colors!' they all said.

'The canopy which is to be held over Your Majesty in the procession is waiting,' announced the Lord High Chamberlain.

'I am quite ready,' announced the Emperor, and he looked at himself again in the mirror, turning from side to side as if carefully examining his handsome attire.

The courtiers who were to carry the train felt about on the ground pretending to lift it: they walked on solemnly pretending to be carrying it. Nothing would have persuaded them to admit they could not see the clothes, for fear they would be thought stupid or unfit for their posts.

And so the Emperor set off under the high canopy, at the head of the great procession. It was a great success. All the people standing by and at the windows cheered and cried, 'Oh, how splendid are the Emperor's new clothes. What a magnificent train! How well the clothes fit!' No one dared to admit that he couldn't see anything, for who would want it to be known that he was either stupid or unfit for his post?

But among the crowds a little child suddenly gasped out, 'But he hasn't got anything on.' And the people began to whisper to one another what the child had said. 'He hasn't got anything on.' 'There's a little child saying he hasn't got anything on.' Till everyone was saying, 'But he hasn't got anything on.' The Emperor himself had the uncomfortable feeling that what they were whispering was only too true. 'But I will have to go through with the procession,' he said to himself.

So he drew himself up and walked boldly on holding his head higher than before, and the courtiers held on to the train that wasn't there at all.

* * *

I wanted you to read this story for a few reasons: You'll see that you are not alone in wanting to live up to the reputation you've created. And we're aware that people have done stupid things for centuries, so that fact that you've wanted to maintain the status quo is nothing new. The emperor, like yourself, insulated himself with people who accepted living a lie rather than admitting something was wrong.

Wake up and smell the manure; it's not roses. Take responsibility for what you've created and/or accepted in your relationship and move on. Misery loves company. The people encouraging you to continue living an illusion have issues themselves or are benefiting from your suffering.

Trust your spirit. It is urging you to seek what God has for you, not what you've given yourself. The greater unknown is where God is, the lesser known is where you have been. You do not have any more time to waste. You can recover money, replace things, but you cannot get back wasted youth, time or lost moments in your life. After reading the story, ask yourself which character you are! Isn't it time you stop playing your part is this life tragedy? Of course it is. Being foolish is one thing, being a fool is another.

Now is your season to be mindful of what you're teaching yourself, let alone your children. You deserve to be happy, loved and fulfilled. It's time to take dominion over your life and get what you have deserved for so long: to be happy and at peace with yourself.

CHAPTER 3

KIDS AND BREAKING UP

MINIMIZING THE EFFECTS ON YOUR CHILDREN

Every year, more than a million children in the United States experience the divorce of their parents. Whether you're married or not, the process and trauma children experience from a breakup normally begins long before you separate. If you're indecisive about breaking up or getting a divorce, please take a close look at what the struggle is doing to your children. Depending on how long you drag it out, parental disagreements, anger, fighting and stress continue to worsen throughout the breakup process. For the sake of yourself and your children, it's very important that you decisively get on with your life. Procrastination is an ally to no one; hesitation compounds the damaging effects that breaking up and divorce have on children.

Children end up in the midst of a fractured relationship in three ways:

- Birthed into it: you and your ex are the adopted or biological parents
- Grafted into it: step-children are involved
- Blended into it: you have a child and so does your ex

In any of these cases, the subject of our discussion is how you affect them, and how they affect you.

Children born into an unhealthy relationship are truly victims of two immature people leaping before looking. On the other hand, some kids are the catalyst for the destruction of a good relationship. Typically children fit into one or two categories: Current victims of, or future catalyst for, divorce. What that means is parenting differences, ex spouses, ex in-laws and strained finances can damage children's security. At the other extreme, children can manipulate the vulnerabilities of an already strained relationship. Though an ugly subject, it is one we must address. But before we begin the process of dismantling this relationship, let's learn to minimize the damage to any children present. What seems to be a curse will transform into a blessing if you do something about your problem right now.

Breaking up is a horrible thing for all parties concerned; nonetheless, we can take lemons and make lemonade out of this situation. This chapter is dedicated to helping you understand that there is a healthy way to handle this situation. Our goal is to help you understand how to shape the thoughts and feelings that your child or children may have while you all survive this breakup. I'm going to provide suggestions to help you communicate with your kids. Believe it or not, how negative your children's reaction is to your break up or divorce directly relates to how you inform them of your decision.

When it is obvious that you cannot put your differences aside and make the marriage work, remaining in a destructive relationship is dangerous to everyone, especially children. Kids are far better off with parents apart, rather than together as it relates to the subject of dysfunctional, necrotic, immature, and hostile relationships. As a parent you set a benchmark for what is 'normal' in your child's mind. Unless something drastic happens, they will subsequently duplicate what they've been taught when they become adults. Staying together for the sake of appearances fools no one. If anything, you are establishing a morally wrong, dishonest mindset for yourself and your offspring. An example is a woman who is battered by a man on a day-in and day-out basis, staying for the sake of the children. She's not helping the child; she's teaching them to tolerate abuse or be abusive. Children learn by example and modeling—not talk. Children learn from what you do, not say.

Here are some reasons why this is a very unhealthy approach. Check out the following:

We'll use a mentally and physically abusive relationship

as an example. Let's pretend that you have a daughter. You're teaching her that it is normal to be hit, called names, or taken for granted. Furthermore, you are providing a template for life that is threatening and rooted in secrecy. In this case, what you don't know may kill your child or grandchildren. Now pretend you have a son, you're licensing him to be a future abuser. You're giving an implied endorsement that it is okay to beat women. The mere fact that you live a lie on a daily basis indoctrinates your children to live an illusion too. The sad, distressing part is that if you keep this up they will think that this is normal, and it's okay to do so. Why not, momma and daddy did it! You are your child's moral compass.

Though stress may blind you to this fact, your child's sense of the world is solely based on what they experience from the lifestyle you provide. Although there are other influences, the most significant influence in any child's life is that of the parent's conduct, especially their behavior toward one another. Who you are dating, engaged to, or spending a great deal of time with has an equal effect on shaping the perceptions of younger children. In addition, kids can suffer from needless trauma and stress when the parents are rude, hostile, loud, violent or threatening toward each other. Compounding this problem, in-laws, relatives and friends who make negative comments about either parent or their families in front of the child create needless tension and anxiety. Such behavior teaches children at any age that there is no stable, secure loving place. Think twice about who and what you allow to influence your kids. Statements cannot be erased from the child's memory. It's the equivalent of being in a court case and telling the jury to disregard the last statement. It may not be part of the transcript, but the fact that the comment was made definitely plays a huge role in the subconscious attitude of jurors and the verdict rendered.

It is imperative that you remember why you're breaking up to begin with. If you're sane, a series of events led you to this decision. Remaining in a relationship for the sake of the child is not only stupid, it's detrimental to the child's self-worth and self-perception. It doesn't matter if it's the woman or the man in a physically or emotionally-abusive relationship, you're setting your child up to see that as the status quo. The negative effects of a breakup are very much controlled by how the parents, caregivers and relatives present things to children.

One sign that you're in an extremely sick and dysfunctional situation is arguing and fighting in front of the kids. When this behavior is carried on by extended families, significant others, caregivers and relatives, it leaves children dazed and confused about what's going on. Despite the age of the child, this is never a good thing. The right thing to do is to talk quietly about your differences without the children ever knowing there is a problem. It is your responsibility to ask the same of family members. However, the worst thing to do is handle things in a quiet manner one moment and argue like to damn fools the next!

Likewise, insist that your relatives also exercise some restraint in voicing their opinions about your mate in the presence of your kids. The long-term effects of either behavior are equally detrimental to the child's sense of self-worth. Remember, in the kid's view you are talking about the half of what makes them who they are.

TELLING CHILDREN ABOUT YOUR BREAKUP

It is very important that you take the time to think carefully. You need to be cautious about how and what you tell your child. It is best, for the sake of the child, that you and your ex talk to them together about your decision. This strategy has one healthy side effect—it will help you to avoid blaming each other for your breakup and force you to focus on the interest of the child.

Here are some tips:

- Set a good time to meet as a family.
- Prior to the meeting, agree on what you're going to tell the child or children.
- Stay calm; check your attitude and emotions at the door.
- Have a third party present to keep things on track, someone whom the child trusts and who is non-biased.

Remember, the younger the child, the more confused and confusing the situation is; this is especially true for ages four through nine. Whatever their age, limit your discussion to the most significant and immediate issues. Kids, regardless of age, can become overwhelmed when given too much information. It is important to emphasize that their basic needs will be met and to the best degree possible, their lifestyle and daily routines will not change. It is also very vital that they know their relationships with both parents will continue, if possible.

Do not give the child a false sense of hope. They need to know that this dissolution is permanent and that it's not their fault. Keep the drama out, especially with younger children. This isn't a time to manipulate or influence the child into taking sides or feeling sorry for you or your ex.

If the child or children are older than age six, ask what concerns and fears they have. Don't pressure them to answer right then; give them time to think about the breakup and the changes that are going to be made. Listen to what they have to say, but do not allow that to influence your decision. It is not unusual for people to try stay in extremely destructive relationships for the sake of children. I strongly caution you: Do not make that mistake! As with leopards and zebras that don't change their spots and stripes, neither do malfunctioning relationships.

If your ex isn't mature enough to rationally discuss this breakup with your children, it still needs to be done. You have no choice but to meet with your child or children alone. You owe them this. When they get older, time will reveal who had their interests at heart. Despite the fact that you may be mad as hell, do your best not to badmouth your ex or their family. Everything that you say or you do will be a reference card for your children later in life. Your job is to be a positive role model. Don't forget that your child will use what you do today as template for tomorrow. This is a time to teach them how be strong and not weak, how to encourage themselves under pressure. They will reap what you sow. Your primary objective is to set an example of how a mature, rational adult handles an ugly, tense situation. Teaching them by example how to respect themselves and others during difficult and tense times.

Your means of handling this sensitive time will either result in very positive or very negative long-term effects. In dysfunctional families respect for authority goes out the window, especially after parents divorce, the reason being that the central authority figures in the children's life could not respect each other, let alone provide a reliable environment for them. Think of it in these terms: If your spouse or yourself could not respect, trust, love and honor each other, what good are the rest of life's rules? The world in which we live today offers a sad but true fact that kids are bombarded with examples of authority figures breaking their own rules. That's why it is imperative that you terminate a horrific, non-healthy relationship as soon as possible. If children cannot find a good example of love at home, where will they find it? It is incumbent that you provide an illustration of a healthy value system.

One of the best things you can do for your child is to provide a nurturing, loving home. Kids learn how to relate to others by watching their parents relate to other people. It is better to break up and demonstrate fortitude and strength to a child rather than remain in an ill-fated relationship. Doing so teaches them to live a lie, and creates a subconscious expectation that love can't be trusted. Kids are much smarter than you think. You may fool yourself, but you can't fool them. Especially teenagers and young adults.

Ugly breakups create insecurity and low self-esteem in kids of all ages. Because of insecurity and low self-esteem, these children are highly vulnerable to joining gangs and other negative peer groups. In view of the fact that their world seems so unstable, it is easy to attach themselves to anyone or group that offers a consistent standard. Like you, kids have a natural desire to prop up their self-esteem. This need to belong affects children in the same way that it does adults. Just as loneliness can inspire you to look for love in all the wrong places, low self-esteem leads kids to seek approval anywhere they can find it. In the case of preteens, adolescents, and young adults, low self-esteem can lead to drug abuse, sexual promiscuity, or inappropriate relationships with other equally-stressed teens or even worse, pedophiles. With boys the temptation to join a gang is multiplied threefold, especially from ages 9 to 15. Sports, faith-based social groups, and mentors can provide a positive alternative.

It is extremely important that you pay attention to the warning signs that your child may present. These signs can range from acting out in school, mistreating siblings, abusing pets, declining grades or even destroying items in the home. This behavior needs to be greeted with compassion and understanding but I caution you not to allow your child to manipulate you because of these broken circumstances. Use this time to strengthen their character, not make excuses for a lack of it.

Even young children as early as age three are capable of manipulating you and your ex. Kids learn triangulation early. When a child doesn't get what they want from one parent, they manipulate the other by lying to or about the other parent. Sometimes they will resort to revealing private details about your life to your ex or telling your ex-in-laws dirt on you just to get their way. It is not unusual for women or men to overcompensate with gifts, extra attention and time to appease the child. Frequently this happens because of one or both parents having a self-imposed guilt trip due to the breakup.

As with most dysfunctional families, the apple does not fall far from the tree. It is in your and your child's best interests to curb such deviant behaviors at their inception. You must teach your children that life is not fair. Just because things, including relationships, don't go their way, does not provide an excuse for unacceptable behavior, disrespectful attitudes, disobedience and talking back. Often parents needlessly tolerate flare-ups and outbursts from children, attributing their behavior to the relationship going bad. Don't blame yourself, spank your bad ass kid. I don't mean abuse your child, but if you spare the rod you will spoil the child.

Enforce the same discipline and rules that you would if you and you ex were still together. If you don't, you will regret it. Children need consistent discipline, structure and good modeling from both parents. It is not uncommon for one or both parents to become Santa Claus with the goal of persuading the child to favor them. Controlling your ex is not possible; but if that's you, it is a very selfish, unhealthy and narcissistic behavior. Such behavior will serve as a catalyst in lowering the child's value system as well as creating feelings of entitlement, resulting in social and behavioral setbacks for you and your child or children.

We cannot take away the discomfort that a breakup or divorce causes children but we can lessen the long-lasting effects this situation can create. I want you to understand that this isn't going to be easy; it will take time and consistency.

Let's start with five easy steps:

- ◆ Utilize appropriate age therapy.
- ◆ Consider their feelings.
- ◆ Pay attention to their moods and behavior.
- ◆ Watch for psychosomatic symptoms (including headaches, tummy aches, not sleeping).
- ◆ Always remain a concerned, compassionate and authoritative parent.

Here is something that I found on The University of Missouri Extension web site which I think can be used as a wonderful aid in helping you understand how to relate to your children's understanding of divorce by age group.[6]

---

[6] The following, to the end of this chapter, is reproduced with slight formatting modification from MU Extension publication GH6600,

Children's Understanding of Divorce by Age Group

Children's understanding of parental divorce depends on their developmental stage. It is important for parents to know what thoughts and feelings children of different ages may be having so that they can modify their own behaviors to help children adjust to the divorce.

INFANTS

Understandings

- Infants notice changes in parents' energy level and emotional state.
- Older infants notice when one parent is no longer living in the home.

Feelings

- More irritability, such as crying and fussing.
- Changes in sleeping, napping and other daily routines.

What parents can do for infants

- Keep normal schedules and routines.
- Reassure infants of your continued presence with physical affection and loving words.
- Keep children's favorite toys, blankets or stuffed animals close at hand.

Helping Children Understand Divorce, with the kind permission of University of Missouri Extension.

TODDLERS

Understandings

- Recognize that one parent no longer lives at home.
- May express empathy toward others, such as a parent who is feeling sad.

Feelings

- May have difficulty separating from parents.
- May express anger toward parent.
- May lose some of the skills they have developed, like toilet training.
- Toddlers may show some of the behaviors that they outgrew, such as thumb sucking.
- Sleeping and nap time routines may change.
- Older toddlers may have nightmares.

What parents can do for toddlers

- Spend more time with children when preparing to separate (e.g., arrive 10 to 15 minutes earlier than usual when you take your child to child care).
- Provide physical and verbal reassurance of your love.
- Show understanding of child's distress; recognize that, given time and support, old behaviors (thumb sucking) will disappear and newly developed skills (toilet training) will reappear.

- Talk with other important adults and caregivers about how to support your child during this transition time.

PRESCHOOL AND EARLY ELEMENTARY CHILDREN

Understandings

- Preschoolers recognize that one parent no longer lives at home.

- Elementary school children begin to understand that divorce means their parents will no longer be married and live together, and that their parents no longer love each other.

Feelings

- Will likely blame themselves for the divorce.

- May worry about the changes in their daily lives.

- Have more nightmares.

- May exhibit signs of sadness and grieving because of the absence of one parent.

- Preschoolers may be aggressive and angry toward the parent they blame.

- Because preschoolers struggle with the difference between fantasy and reality, children may have rich fantasies about parents getting back together.

What parents can do for preschool and early elementary children

- Repeatedly tell children that they are not responsible for the divorce.

65

- Reassure children of how their needs will be met and of who will take care of them.
- Talk with children about their thoughts and feelings; be sensitive to children's fears.
- Plan a schedule of time for children to spend with their other parent. Be supportive of children's ongoing relationship with the other parent.
- Read books together about children and divorce (See list.)
- Gently, and matter-of-factly, remind children that the divorce is final and that parents will not get back together again.

PRETEENS AND ADOLESCENTS

Understandings

- Understand what divorce means but may have difficulty accepting the reality of the changes it brings to their family.
- Although thinking at a more complex level, still may blame themselves for the divorce.

Feelings

- May feel abandoned by the parent who moves out of the house.
- May withdraw from long-time friends and favorite activities.
- May act out in uncharacteristic ways (start using bad language, become aggressive or rebellious).

- May feel angry and unsure about their own beliefs concerning love, marriage, and family.
- May experience a sense of growing up too soon.
- May start to worry about adult matters, such as the family's financial security.
- May feel obligated to take on more adult responsibilities in the family.

What parents can do for preteens and adolescents

- Maintain open lines of communication with children; reassure children of your love and continued involvement in their lives.
- Whenever possible, both parents need to stay involved in children's lives, know children's friends, what they do together, and keep up with children's progress at school and in other activities.
- Honor family rituals and routines (Sunday dinner, weeknight homework time, grocery shopping together, watching favorite television shows or movies as a family).
- If you need to increase children's household responsibilities, assign chores and tasks that are age-appropriate (help with laundry, housecleaning, yard work, meal preparations); show appreciation for children's contributions.
- Avoid using teenagers as confidants; plan special time for yourself with adult friends and family

members.

◆ Tell children who will be attending special occasions such as sporting events and graduation ceremonies, especially if you plan to take a new romantic partner.

* * *

USING BOOKS TO TALK WITH CHILDREN ABOUT DIVORCE

Children's books about divorce can help them work through the issues they face. Reading books can give children a way to express their emotions and discuss issues that they may not otherwise be comfortable talking about. These books may also help parents understand children's experiences of divorce.

◆ *It's Not Your Fault, KoKo Bear.* Vicky Lansky (1998). Book Peddlers. This book is designed for parents and children ages 3 to 5 years to read together. Each page provides a large picture to show what is happening in the story and includes messages for parents. The messages for parents help make a connection between the story and what happens to children in real families. KoKo Bear faces situations that help him learn what divorce means, and that he is not to blame for the divorce. He is helped to talk about his feelings, and is told that he is still loved by both parents.

◆ *Dinosaurs Divorce: A guide for changing families.*

Laurene Krasney Brown and Marc Brown (1986). Little Brown and Company. This award-winning book is designed for parents and young school-aged children to read together. Stories are presented in a cartoon strip pattern and organized around topics that are important for children experiencing the divorce of their parents. Issues such as why parents divorce, living with one parent, having two homes, telling friends, parents' new partners, and celebrating special occasions are discussed. Solutions to problems that may come up are illustrated by the actions of the dinosaur children and their parents.

◆ *How Do I Feel About: My parents' divorce.* Julia Cole (1997). Copper Beach Books. This book is written for older school-aged children with some reading skills, but should be read at least the first time with a parent so that the child may ask questions. Topics covered in the book include: why divorce happens, difficult feelings, and feeling okay. Photographs and cartoon illustrations show that everyone lives in a unique situation. The book reassures children that they are not alone in having their parents divorce and that there is more than one way that problems may be solved.

◆ *Pre-Teen Pressures: Divorce.* Debra Goldentyer (1998). Steck-Vaughn Company. This book, written for pre-teen readers, covers a wide range of issues. It is recommended that parents read it before reading it with their children. This book discusses common changes that take place for divorcing families. A variety of families are presented to show that there are many reasons why marriages end (affairs, violence/abuse and alcoholism). A variety of family stories are used to show that individuals adjust differently, make different decisions and move on to new relationships at different speeds. The children's roles in their own adjustment to divorce are emphasized.

A BOOK FOR PARENTS

◆ *Making Divorce Easier on Your Child: 50 Effective Ways to Help Children Adjust.* Nicholas Long and Rex Forehand (2002). Contemporary Books. This book provides practical, effective advice for parents on dealing with issues including talking to children about divorce, managing stress, communicating with the child's other parent, single parenting, and building a support network. It is clearly written and organized so that parents can quickly find information about specific issues.

Knowledge is power. What you don't know can hurt you and your kids. Educate yourself. You don't have to do this alone. How you handle this has long-term effects on you and your offspring. If you neglect your needs, or theirs, that is not a good thing. Using support groups, clergy and trained counselors will make this transition better for all parties concerned. Handle this right so you can focus on your needs. Children will only be whole if you are.

REFERENCES

Amato, P. 1994. Life-span Adjustment of Children to their Parents' Divorce. In Children and Divorce, 4 (1). Packard Foundation.

Behrman, R.E. and L. Quinn. 1994. Children and Divorce: Overview and Analysis. In Children and Divorce, 4 (1). Packard Foundation.

Blakeslee, Ives, S. D. Fassler and M. Lash. 1994. The Divorce Workbook. Burlington, VT: Waterfront Books.

Cummings, E.M. and P. Davis. 1994. Children and Marital Conflict. N.Y.: Guilford Press.

Meyer, Cathy. How To Keep Divorce From Having Long Lasting Effects on Children. http://divorcesupport.about.com/od/childrenanddivorce/ht/effectsonchild.htm

Mulroy, M., C.Z. Malley, R.M. Sabatelli and R. Waldron. 1995. Parenting Apart: Strategies for effective co-parenting. Storrs, CT: University of Connecticut Cooperative Extension System.

Stevenson, M.R., and K.N. Black. 1996. How Divorce Affects Offspring: A research approach. Boulder, CO: Westview Press.

University of Missouri Extension. Helping Children Understand Divorce. http://extension.missouri.edu/ publications/DisplayPub.aspx?P=GH6600

Way2Hope.org. Effects of Divorce on Children. www.way2hope.org/ effects_of_divorce_on_children.htm

CHAPTER 4

IT'S YOUR TIME

GETTING YOURSELF BACK TOGETHER

'If I had known then what I know now!' Sound familiar? There's no better time than the present to take control of your life. Knowing who, what, when, where, why, and how to take charge is the key to a successful life. Applying the right tactics, at the right time, prevents set backs but, before today, not doing so caused your life to turn into a battlefield. You war against principalities in high places. The high places I'm referring to are your mind and the minds of other people. Taming every wild, illusionary and disobedient thought is essential in releasing yourself to fulfill your destiny. Implementing sound strategies and developing a logical thought process are the most effective weapons on the mind's battlefield. Critical thinking skills are pivotal in formulating a joyful and productive life, and when these are accompanied by a proactive decision-making process, confronting life's issues will make you, not break you. At the end of this chapter, you are going to possess and control the armaments you need to be successful at life.

From this day forward, your level of contribution and commitment will determine how successful you become. In the past, repercussions from other people were a major source of your frustrations, rejections, bewilderment and defeats, i.e. your ex, your relatives and so-called friends. Those excuses no longer exist. Now, you are at the helm of your life. Favorable outcomes aren't caused by, nor hindered by, the actions of other people. Frustrating, overwhelming, perplexed feelings that held you hostage in the past will stop happening if you consistently use techniques addressed in this chapter.

Later in this section you will find a list of how-to steps and resources that are foolproof. Here's where we address everything you need to get your thought process and life on track. Eliminate the excuses and wasted time due to someone else's influence on your decisions. Success is yours if you don't quit. Without further ado, the time starts right now.

A LESSON FROM CHILDHOOD

When I was a child one of my fondest playtime memories

was being told, 'It's your turn.' I don't know about you, but I recall how good I felt when my chance arrived to do whatever. Knowing that I was going next revved me up. Well, guess what? It's your time. You have survived a great deal and it's time to start reaping the fruits of your labor. Any setbacks or failures that occur from this moment forward can be attributed to the fact you gave up or simply didn't try hard enough. Commit this to memory: The world doesn't owe you anything. However, you do owe yourself, your family and the people God put in your path something: They deserve the best you that you can be. When you were a child, you thought as a child; now you're an adult and it's time to put away childish things. In other words, the pity party time is over.

I want you to close your eyes, and open your mind, put a big smile on your face, and shout, 'It's my turn!' Don't worry about making a fool out of yourself, looking or sounding crazy. You've already done that several times before; however, on this occasion it's for a good reason. We're getting ready to take a trip, so pack your mind and let's go. You, and I are on our way to that special place inside of you. Go boldly forward. Sit down, and shut everything and everyone out. You must do this alone. After all, this is a hallowed, sacred place because we're dealing with the inner sanctuary where your spirit lives.

It's time to become acquainted with your spirit and explore what's housed deep inside you. During moments like this, I suggest you sit by the water, go to the park or get a glass of your favorite beverage and just chill. Turn off all external stimuli, put on a blindfold or simply close your eyes. (Just make sure you are somewhere safe and secure.) Imagine yourself doing what you were created to do. Doing that which results in your being happy, fulfilled, needed and loved. Do this over the next few days, weeks and months, if necessary. Your instincts will let you know when you have arrived; be prepared to return accompanied by the real you. For some people this takes hours. For others it takes weeks, or even months. Don't rush it. Though the vision tarried, it is coming to pass. You can continue the other activities in the chapter while you perfect this.

This time around, you're not going to fail for lack of a plan. God has a tailor-made formula for your life and it cannot fail. However, there is a catch: You must take your turn at life. One must take risk in life or I guarantee there will be no reward. So get off your behind. It's time to begin the work. Faith without works is dead!

Back to my childhood we go. I left out a few things. Each time my turn came, I wasn't always a success. Sometimes, I blew it. Naturally, I didn't feel so hot when I did. Nonetheless, I learned from my mistakes. No matter what I was unsuccessful in, or what I failed at, my mistakes made me a stronger person. You have my guarantee that it will turn out the same way for you. Every dark cloud has a silver lining. I didn't give up, because I knew that eventually I would succeed and when I did you couldn't tell me anything.

That's when the light came on. I had an Oprah moment! Finally, I realized that failing didn't mean that I was a failure; nor did losing mean that I was a loser. It is part of the process. Life is a process, not an event. Loss is a tool that God uses to teach you wisdom, tenacity, perseverance, grace and patience. When viewed properly, losing isn't such a bad thing. It's just another tool life uses to humble and groom you. Not to mention that it makes victory that much sweeter.

As a child, playing games is fun when you win! When I was a kid I hated losing. Even as an adult, I think losing is rotten. But, the more mature I got, a reality sat in. I learned, 'You cannot win them all.' It took a while, but I learned the real joy comes from learning that it's a blessing to participate in the game.

WINNING AT LIFE

Though it is to be enjoyed, life isn't a game and neither is love. Just the same, you can't triumph at either unless you participate. It is a fact that 'love' is the only game. (Though, I have to note that love isn't a game, only a figure of speech.) Two people can play and both lose. With that stated we are going to work at this love thing. Love is a power. Let's begin by teaching you to love yourself. Love will empower you! God is Love! The first step is learning to love yourself and everything that's going right in your life.

Isn't it about time that you appreciated the simple things in life? Money, toys, cars, clothes and shoes may bring you temporary happiness but they cannot comfort you when you're going through hell. The best things in life are free, such as, laughing out loud, making a silly mistake and laughing at yourself, not judging others or feeling judged, or just being in a good mood for the sake of being happy. I am here to tell you, you've attained the point in this book that confirms you are well on your way. Still, you must do the work. Faith without works is dead. As you get ready to embrace the real you, keep in mind that to whom much is given, much shall be required.

God created a perfect you, flaws and all. Eyes have not seen, nor ears heard the goodness that God has for you. However, as with all good things, there are a few requirements. Nothing in life just happens, except death. Victory requires effort, accountability and strategy. This chapter is about climbing the stairway to success.

Winning at life is ensured when you have a plan. Ten steps will assure success:

- Don't go backwards
- Trade in change for transformation
- Cut ties with all negative influences
- Create a realistic agenda
- Put dates on your goals
- Establish healthy new relationships
- Stop procrastinating, take a fresh step daily
- Set milestones, do your best to reach them
- Enjoy all of the journey, including the Highs and Lows
- Embrace the motto: Failure is not an option

This is easier done than said. That isn't a typo. It takes more effort to live a non-fulfilling failure than it does to embrace a success-filled life. Living a life composed of stress, hostility and mediocrity requires your going out of your way to put up with a lot of unnecessary, negative mess. This encompasses accepting things such as, living in a stress-filled home, remaining accustomed to tension and hostility, and, last but not least, living in mediocrity and misery on a daily basis. If you're a damn fool, that should sound enticing. However, the real you has been there, done that.

Aren't you sick and tired, of being sick, and tired? This morning I heard Pastor Creflo Dollar say, 'Mediocrity is the best of the worst, and the worst of the best.' In chapter one, I told you about that long, boring funeral I attended. What I didn't tell you was that the man was rude and arrogant; nobody liked him. During the majority of his life, he didn't achieve anything. He had a job working for his father but the problem with that is his old man didn't do anything. (Some of you will catch that in a minute, for the rest of us keep reading.)

My point is, nobody celebrates a life of mediocrity. The two hours I spent at that man's funeral was the equivalent of watching a rock age. To this day, my only regret was that I didn't leave sooner or that I went at all. That's how you should feel about staying in a stale, musty, non-productive relationship. Living in the past is not a good thing.

Only an anthropologist, historian or archeologist

benefits from living in the past. For the record, they only work in it, they don't dwell there. The future happens when you consistently choose to leave your past in the past, and the people from it alone.

DISCOVER YOUR OWN PROMISED LAND

Fulfilling your destiny requires seeking and discovering your purpose. Another way to say this is, leave the mountain and head to the Promised Land. Just like the story in the Bible, there will be those who become comfortable with the status quo. Although God sustained them with manna and quail, that wasn't all He wanted them to have. They became so accustomed to surviving, they confused it with living. You were created to have life, and life more abundantly. As with some of the Israelites, you and some of your friends, choose to stay stuck where you are because it is not in your or their selfish interest for things to change. But you are not them. Get the hell out of there and get on with your life before it's too late.

Choosing to live the life you deserve simply requires embracing and being committed to fulfilling your purpose. If you do that, the fruits are sure to come. You have to choose a lifestyle based on commitment, wisdom, focus and perseverance. Companionship, love, peace, joy and happiness are not the keys to success, they are the fruits of it. This is the place where you make a decision to look forward and not back.

The first step in this transformation is coming to grips

with the fact that you cannot go backwards. The lesser known is where you have been, the greater unknown is where God and your future are. He who began a good work in you will see it through to its very perfection. This season requires confidence in yourself. Mistakes are going to happen, but that is to be expected. All mistakes become blessings, provided that you turn your bloopers into life lessons. Nobody is perfect, but you must keep striving toward perfection.

Are you a necrophiliac? Necrophilia is being in love with dead things. Do you want a new life or a dying situation? How long can you serve two masters? Sooner than later, you will betray one for the other. It takes a person with a made-up mind to achieve anything. Ask yourself if you are tired of going round and round in circles, only to wind up right back where you started. In the story of Moses and the Israelites, a twelve-day journey ended up taking forty years because a few people feared change. That's correct, the Israelites endured forty years of unnecessary turmoil because they allowed their leaders to keep them in a sub-standard comfort zone. Their justification was, their clothes didn't tear and manna and quail fell from the sky every day. Some of them took that as a sign that God had reached his plateau. The God I serve can do better than some clothes, a two-piece chicken dinner and a biscuit every day.

Isn't it sad how we limit ourselves, then, turn around and limit God too? The truth is the Israelites allowed a few cowardly leaders to block an entire nation's blessing. Who are you allowing to block your blessings? What excuses are you using to limit yourself? This happened to them because they feared change or simply did not want to do the work. They began to live a lie in a false comfort zone. Don't allow this to happen to you. It's a shame if you allow other people's hidden agendas and complacency to negatively impact your life.

The lesson here is to never accept another person's status quo but do what's good for you. When a hog gets stuck in the mud, he's right at home. Let the same thing happen to a sheep. The sheep can't function, it doesn't feel comfortable. What's a natural state for one is a wake-up call to another. Are you a sheep or a swine? I think you got the picture. I read somewhere, 'My sheep hear my voice.' For those of you who are non-Christian, that is another way of saying that we should learn to hear God's voice. Listen to your spirit. Don't cast your pearls before swine.

The Promised Land is where transformation occurs. The catch is you must seize your blessing. Follow that little voice inside you, it will serve as a guide. It is the same voice, had you heeded it a long time ago, that would have helped you arrive here much sooner. Don't sweat it. There is still time and you are here now and that's what matters most. Your spirit is guiding you toward the next step. I realize that this season in your life can be intimidating, so I'm going to give you some signs to look for. They will help you to distinguish that voice from your ego and provide confirmation that you're on the right track:

1. If God gives you a vision, he will make provision.

2. Effort will be required, but there will be little resistance.

3. Prayer will provide confirmation.

4. Circumstances will line up with your vision.

The innate talents you possess will bring you before great men, so don't go looking for them. Instead, be aware that now is the time to get everything ready:

◆ Study

◆ Train

◆ Practice

◆ Prepare yourself

I caution you, if you have not perfected those God-given gifts, failure is imminent. Just because you have been doing something for years, take it to another level.

MEETING YOUR DESTINY

Preparation meeting opportunity is the first step toward destiny. Creation of an agenda is key in your process. The gifts you possess are unique to you, but you need to fine-tune them. Don't feel discouraged if you haven't unearthed your gift yet. Everyone is endowed with a special gift, something that they are naturally good at. Your gifts will make room for you and your talents will bring you before great men.

The skills God blessed you with will be a major factor in taking control over your life. Write down some things that you do extremely well. These are the things that do not require struggle, nor do they create a great deal of stress when you do them. Keep it real and the more you do whatever you're created to do, the more you love it.

It's likely that your talent is whatever you've been doing well most of your life. Another proof is that your gift recognized by anyone that comes in contact with it. Another sign is it validates your life, and is a blessing to other people. Whatever that thing is, that's your gift. Some people have the gift of listening, others the gift of speaking, and yet others the gift of art or teaching or motivation. No matter what your talent is, seek it out and you will find your purpose. That which you seek is equally seeking you.

After you identify your talent, I strongly suggest that you begin perfecting that ability by continuing your education. A legitimate trade school, a junior college, or traditional institution is a wonderful place to start. For some of you it means getting your GED, for others it could be starting a new profession, getting a masters degree, or taking a series of continuing education classes at a legitimate university—stay away from over-priced quickie trade schools that are a rip-off and typically not accredited—but whatever the case, take your first step. Wasted time is a friend to no one.

<u>Finding your destiny is the first step.</u> It goes hand in hand with discovering your purpose: as you pursue and complete the work, you will start seeing the vision. Time and effort are going to reveal the picture. Write it down and start making it plain. This is done by monitoring your progress and sticking to a realistic plan.

Making a plan is the second step. Fulfilling your part is a must. God's way of identifying you is by your talents and your talent will fit your personality and abilities like a glove. However, benefiting from it requires that you create a workable plan. Not doing so is the equivalent of praying for a job and not taking the time to fill out an application. I doubt seriously that you will hear a knock at the door one day and when you ask, 'Who is it?' the response will be, 'Hi, I'm your job.' God feeds the birds every day, but He doesn't throw worms in their nest. Receiving an inheritance requires two things: that you claim your blessing and that you be 'the real you.' In other words, you must be the authentic and deliberately pursue your destiny. That requires that your actions and attitudes be consistent. That is the only way to successfully validate your identity.

TRANSFORMING YOUR PLAN THROUGH D.A.T.E.

A goal transforms into a plan when you use a four-letter word: D. A. T. E. In this case, D stands for determination; A for assertive; T for tenacity; and E for effort. A date serves a few purposes:

1. It helps you determine how well you are doing, as it relates to your goal.

2. It gives you an indicator of how strong your commitment is.

3. It gives you a valid reason to celebrate where you are in achieving your objective.

I stated earlier that this journey isn't merely about reaching the destination, it is also about connecting with the journey. Nothing in this world can be done without the assistance of good people. Creating positive, healthy relationships along the way is a main ingredient for success toward any endeavor. Ask any successful person, 'Did you do it alone?' The answer will be 'No.' At birth, someone had to help you get here; at death, someone helps you leave. It is only natural, during the course of your life, that you will need good people. To attract these people you must have strong character and integrity.

While developing productive relationships with the right people, make sure that you form them for the right reasons. Good relationships don't just happen. For the record, this chapter is not about focusing on the romantic aspects of your life. This is about becoming that which you seek in someone else. If you were to meet the perfect mate and you're still screwed up, what good would that do? You would blow it again. We will talk about finding a new lover when you understand how to value all relationships and know what love really is. Our goal, at present, is to change the reason and the way you form all relationships. This chapter focuses on platonic, social and professional relationships with other people. There is a lot more to you than being romance-obsessed. It's time that you became all of what God created you to be.

Let's begin with finding new friends selectively. Only fools go to a new school or job and start claiming everyone as a friend. I remember my dad teaching me that friendly is one thing and friends are another. The world has changed a great deal in the last twenty years. A letter that took several days to go from one person to another a couple of decades ago can now arrive via email in milliseconds. Kids have cell phones. Our cars do everything from telling us how to get places to serving as an extension of the living room. It is no wonder that people have become so isolated. The Internet has replaced going to the club, the mall and even the church. That is both good and bad. As it relates to you, it's great. Because our culture has become so niche-oriented, you can engage with people who share the same interests as you. There are many benefits in that, but pitfalls as well.

Now before you start turning into Ms. or Mr. Congeniality, let's consider where, who, why and how you're to go about making new acquaintances. Predators are out there, so watch yourself. Realize the big difference between being friendly and being friends. A good friendship should be based on something other than the fact that you are at the same place at the same time. One must find some other reason or purpose in forming a relationship with another person.

I teach my clients a philosophy: If a poor man is in the presence of a king, he becomes royal. If a wise man is in the presence of a fool, he is subject to foolishness. In other words, you take on the traits and behavior of those with whom you associate. Also, you're subject to either benefit or be cursed by what accompanies them. Stay away from people who have no character, ambition, principals, or morals.

Ask yourself, why are you seeking this person's friendship, and why are they seeking yours? What do the two of you have in common? Is what you share a good or destructive thing? Have you taken to time to observe how this individual treats other people, and why the treat them that way? Are your value systems alike? Is there evidence that suggests your new potential buddy can be trusted? Does this person have character? Do they possess integrity? The same qualities you seek in a mate must be sought in your friends. Moreover, are these qualities in you? You are whom you associate with. Moreover, they are a big part of you. A chain is only as strong as its weakest link. This time around you need to be the weakest link in your chain.

Yes, that sounds like a lot to require of a new associate. Well, duh! This is a season in which quality beats quantity. It takes time to cultivate good associates. You must be that which you seek or you are going to wind up in the same mess as before, by inviting into your life a bunch of fake, trifling folks who are there for every reason but the right ones. Misery will always love company.

The downside to this character-oriented approach is it takes more than a minute to build a new social network. However, the fantastic part is that if you do it this way, you will develop quality relationships that endure. You are whom you associate with so associate with positive, proactive people. Don't let anyone postpone your progress. Momentum is hard to build and easy to hinder.

Procrastination is the key to failure. The best ideas are useless until you act on them; merely talking about success won't create it. An old American Indian saying states, 'Everybody wants to go to Heaven, but nobody wants to die.' In order for the new you to live, the old you must die. Good and evil cannot live together in peace. Out-of-date ideas will not be effective in today's world. You would look like a damn fool if you tried to light a flat-top stove with a match. That is what procrastination will do. Delaying, postponing or putting off doing the right thing is just as bad as not doing anything at all. The solution to the procrastination problem is two four-letter words:

T I M E and D A T E

Setting a time and date creates milestones. A milestone is the only effective way to track progress using landmarks, benchmarks and achievement. It is the only tangible way to determine significant change or determine the stage you're in as it relates to your goal. I caution you to be patient with yourself. Life is about the journey. You are not, nor will you ever be, perfect. Things don't always go according to plan. The universe has a way of correcting your mistakes. Often we interpret these corrections as delays or road blocks when in fact it is God correcting your timing. He knows the best moment for things to happen in your life. So whenever you experience a setback, an obstacle, or a delay, ask yourself, 'Is God trying to tell me something?' Often He speaks through the voice of circumstances. Typically that happens when you fail to heed the 'signs' or listen to the people who were placed in your life. Success isn't about the destination, it's about the journey.

You may feel lonely, but you are not alone.

CHAPTER 5

ALONE BUT NOT LONELY

COPING WITH SEPARATION

Alone is one thing, lonely is another. Don't feel bad if over the last few days, weeks and months, it seems as though you are kicking everybody to the curb or cutting off your family for a moment. Your spirit knows what you need and when you need it the most. The subconscious is positioning you for resurrection. Despite what others are probably thinking, you have not lost your mind, nor are you tripping. Know it or not, instinctively you've been blocking yourself from intrusion for a reason. How could you think clearly when people, places and things continually interfere? To successfully transform your life, some me-time is desperately needed. That is why your spirit and God have you in a cocoon. You may feel alone and a bit lonely but, when this is over, it will make sense. Your life is in a state of transformation.

God wants all of you to Himself for a reason. He can't communicate with you properly if your attention is divided. When I wrote *Tired of Being Alone*, I realized that being alone, lonely and loneliness were three very different things. All of them serve a unique and special purpose during such times. This is the time that you learn about, and get to know, the real you. You are going to become authentic during this season. The things and people you seek in life will manifest as you develop integrity and character. That process begins with discovering who, what and why you have become the way you are. We are going to explore what molded you into the person you are today.

This chapter is dedicated to discovering whom you were created to be and where things went wrong. There is an old saying, 'As long as you keep your mouth shut, nobody will know how big a fool you truly are.' I've got news for you. If you don't speak up, how will you know what needs to be fixed? With that said, we are going to stop making fools out of ourselves. There is nothing worse than impersonating yourself. It's time to disappear from people for a moment and work on yourself. I promise when you resurface, folks won't recognize you.

We will focus on many ideas in this chapter but the one thing they have in common is you. To construct the real you, we must dissect the person you've become. You're so many things to so many people that some days do you wonder who you are? I'm willing to bet that little, if any, attention has been focused on you lately. With that stated, this is the season for deep thinking and time to ask the hard question: Who are you? By now you're probably a bit confused, maybe even frustrated by that question.

Typically the answer starts generically with your name, where you're from, your age, gender etc. This time we're going far deeper than that. I want you to ask yourself, 'Who am I for real? Why do I do think the way I do? Why do I do the things I do?' If you are like most people, it is difficult as heck to answer that. Here is a hint: Part of it is rooted in your past, another part is in your environment and the last piece is you.

This may be hard to believe now, but at the end of this chapter, every self-destructive thought process that is hindering your life will be under your control. You may not change them immediately, but you will know what they are and where they came from. No longer will destructive feelings, theories, assessments, opinions and views be lurking around, sabotaging your life.

The person you are today is a cumulation of everything that you have seen, heard, felt, thought, hoped for, feared, failed and succeeded at. You're a walking mystery, an enigma that we are going to go over with a fine-tooth comb. Everyone's life is composed of good and bad experiences, but what you do with them makes the difference. What you know about yourself makes all the difference in how you relate to others. In general, people perish for a lack of knowledge. Imagine how much worse that is when you have little, if any, understanding about yourself. If all you know about yourself is what you have experienced, what others have said, or what has been written about you on pieces of paper, you don't know very much about yourself. To fix the behaviors that impair your life, we must understand your life.

Empowerment comes from learning the truth about yourself. Now it's time to learn what makes you tick. Examine the factors in your past that shaped your frame of reference. Without that information the past has the power to hold your future hostage. Half of the problem in getting your head on straight is having a scant knowledge of why you're the way you are.

Example: Imagine you have to be somewhere at six p.m. every day and you are consistently late. Now you have gotten fired again. It's another day and the right time is five o'clock p.m. The sun is setting, the five o'clock news is on. However, three people around you keep telling you, 'It's twelve noon.' You have every indication that something is not right but seldom do you leave your environment. Moreover, these folks happen to be your aunt, friend and cousin. Why wouldn't you respect and value their opinions? But, here is the problem: They purchased defective watches from the same shady person, your mother. Your grandmother gave these watches to your mother to sell when she was a child because your grandmother was a hustler. Out of fear of lost inheritance, loyalty and dysfunction nobody questioned your grandmother. Now, you are scared to question your mother (a generational curse well at work, despite the fact they see that your mother is late for everything she does and keeps getting fired). Aside from that fact, you grew up seeing her get fired for coming to work four to five hours late every day. You justified it because it's your mother. She has the right intentions, great skills, and tries to keep a job. People have told her that she needs to get a new watch, but she isn't hearing it. Your mother's excuse is, 'My momma gave me these watches.'

Now, all of you keep getting terminated, because you're just like your mother, you're always late. The problem is that nobody's willing to tell Mama these out-of-date watches don't work. Your, your aunt's and your cousin's watches have the same malfunction. Now your excuse is your watch was gift from grandmother. You've allowed fear, pride and tradition to stop you from speaking up. Although you have the five o'clock news giving you the correct time, and a clock with the right time at work, you've been fired over and over but you don't have the courage to tell everybody: 'Something is wrong. We're wrong! It's not the boss, the job or the network news, you are wrong! These Mickey Mouse watches haven't worked in years.' Your excuse is, 'Even a broken watch is right twice a day.' As stupid as this story sounds, most of your dysfunctional actions result from what you've seen and heard from poor role models when you were growing up.

In lieu of fact that half of your problem may be rooted in your past, the other half of the transformation problem is not knowing what you need to do to fix your self-defeating behaviors. Knowing how something got broken and the extent of the damage is key to fixing anything. This is especially true when it is applied to healing a broken person. At any rate, if we are going to unshackle you, that is the very information we need.

EXAMINING YOUR LIFE

Before you to embark on this journey, let's sojourn and discover the magnificent, phenomenal person you were birthed to be. One benefit to being a fully-broken person is that we can use all of those fractured pieces to put you back together again. Believe it or not, it takes all those pieces to finally become the real you. In the previous chapters I said, 'Only a fool begins a journey without first assessing the cost.' We are going to begin by assessing what life has cost you, and the price others paid to create your mindset.

Go get a few sheets of paper. Let's start writing down a few things. Begin by describing the situation that you were birthed in. I don't mean what hospital. Explore the circumstances that were present prior to your conception and at the time of your birth. Was it a two-parent or single-family home? Did you have a nurturing or estranged environment as a toddler? Were you born in poverty or with a silver spoon in your mouth? Are your parents sane or strange? Are you adopted? If so, is it by strangers or within your biological family? Were you reared by everybody or by mom and dad, or perhaps it was your grandparents, maybe even an aunt and uncle? Don't try to justify, just tell the facts. This information is extremely important, so take your time, we have a great deal to examine. That is just the tip of the iceberg. Examining your origins is a huge piece of this puzzle.

Next, I want you to examine you life from age three and stop at age seven. Begin doing this alone, if you can, though often people need help recapturing those moments. If you need to, reach out and ask someone who can give you an unbiased view of your early childhood. Examine the surroundings and conditions in which you lived. How were you treated? Were you allowed to have a childhood or were you helping make baby bottles at age five or six? Did your caregivers shield you from the cold cruel world, or were you exposed to things that no little kid should see? Were you aware of sex, domestic violence or illegal drugs? Did your parents divorce or have an unstable relationship? Was there a death of someone very close to you? Was your family economically challenged in any way? Did your family move frequently?

Now examine your life from age nine to fifteen. Did you enter puberty early or late? That means, if you're a female, when did you start your cycle, develop breasts or become sexually active before your peers? If you are a male, when did you experience your growth spurt, grow facial hair or have sex? Were you involved in socially-engaging activities such as sports, music or social organizations and were you good, bad or average? Did your caregivers, family or friends criticize you or support you consistently? Were you told you were loved? If you made mistakes, were you criticized by your caregivers, friends or schoolmates? Were your caregivers permissive, absent, strict, hypocrites, or did they break up? Was your caregiver, father or mother promiscuous? Did you have conservative or liberal role models? Were you in a racially sensitive environment? Think before you answer. It may be necessary that you have two sets of opinions, one for how you perceive things now and another based on how you perceived things then. Don't be surprised if it's both.

You're almost done. Now write down the four most significant events and how they affected your life. These events will include deaths, births, personal failures or achievements and the like. This isn't a time to lie to yourself. Again, tell it like it is. Get some tissues because, done right, some painful memories may surface. On the other hand, some really cool ones will come to mind, too. Everyone is different. Your experiences are unique to you. The goal is to be as honest with yourself as possible. Write down how you feel. Tell the truth about how these events affected your life, both now and then.

Last, but not least, write down what you've experienced during the last three years. Don't focus on other people. Make this about you. What big decisions have you made? How many projects did you start and not finish? Include things like school, personal goals, (losing weight, breaking habits, relocation, etc.) behavioral changes (being abused, abusing others, smoking weed, going to jail, kicking the cat, gossiping, etc.). How successful were you? Did you complete any of your objectives? How many sex partners have you had? (Definition of sex: If your genitalia got touched or seen, or you touched or saw someone else's naughty bits, it's a sexual act.) How many relationships have you had? How many jobs have you had? Keep it real, there are no right or wrong, good or bad answers here.

Whew! By now, it probably feels like you've written a mini autobiography about yourself. You have. If it took more than a day to write, don't be surprised. That's a sign you are taking yourself and your homework seriously. Hint: You will get out of this exercise what you put in it. Often, many revelations take center stage doing this exercise. I want you to take the time to notice a few things:

- God has always placed someone in your life, at the right place, at the right time
- No matter how bad or good things were, you're still here
- Everything that was meant to destroy you wound up blessing you
- You have learned from your mistakes, reading this book is proof,
- Your spirit never left you, no matter how many mistakes you made
- There is still time to fix your life

One day, Mr. or Mrs. Right will come along. At the right time, you need to share this information with them. Nobody can love a caricature. As an authentic person, the negative and positive events in the past are the pearls in your life's necklace.

Don't cast your pearls before swine. I caution you, before sharing intimate details about your life with anyone, make sure it's the right person. Let it be someone that you know for some time. People can use such details to manipulate your feelings, provoke guilt trips and, if they are immature, they will throw your past in your face at the worst time. If it's the right person, they will learn that you are a human being with feelings and a past. Another benefit is that, if it's the right person, they can assist you in spotting your recurrent negative behaviors. That will help you avoid making the same mistakes twice.

Information contained on those pieces of paper answer the question of who you are. That doesn't mean that is all you will ever be. Nonetheless, it will establish what has contributed to your current perceptions of life. Previous seeds sown have a direct correlation to your perspective on life and how you react to problems today. People, places and circumstances contribute to the actions and attitudes that have fashioned your current thought process.

PROACTIVE STRATEGIES

Whether you know it or not, you're one big walking reaction to stimuli. Every experience is a component that you consciously or subconsciously use to devise coping strategies. Thought process is the source of strategies. They're what you use to formulate the tactics for living your life. It is time to become proactive, not reactive. Never is it wise to live life on autopilot.

An example of this is speaking to people early in the morning. It is not uncommon for someone to say, 'Good morning, how's your day going?' Your reply is, 'Good morning—great.' Chances are you could have said, 'Good morning, I had breakfast with the devil.' Does anyone ever stop and really listen to the answer? No! Now it's time to stop hearing and start listening to what's going on with and around you.

If your life is composed of negativity, now you know why you have had the issues you do. Examining anecdotal information explains why you perceive life the way you do. Take the time to read what you wrote. Listen to what is being said. Consider the impact that each event had on your life and the perceptions you formulated based on these events. Remember, perception is reality. This is the moment in which you transform your truth. If your life has been filled with engaging and positive experiences, you should realize that you are truly blessed. Certainly that is not the case for the majority of people. Nonetheless, how you use those experiences will serve as a catalyst for transformation in your life. Understanding the past empowers you to change the future. This chapter is dedicated to that power.

ALONE AND IN CONTROL

Take a good look at what the word 'alone' means. As an adjective, it means 'having no one else present.' As an adverb, it suggests that something is confined to a specified subject. Relating to you, it indicates a benchmark for your life. Once and for all, you are taking time to be alone with yourself. God finally has your full attention. He has you to himself. Take a good look at yourself. The act of looking with your eyes suggests that an object is in your field of vision, but if you 'see' at an object, you view things at a much deeper level. When someone asks if you understand a fact and you do, you say 'Oh, now I see.' To 'see' something means that you understand it. Now is the time to focus on yourself and truly see who you are.

Now that you're finally in control of your life, what are you expecting from yourself?

- ◆ What are you searching for?
- ◆ What have you learned about you?
- ◆ What lies have you been living?
- ◆ What truths have you found?

At this stage being alone with yourself is necessary. Don't panic, it's only for a little while. Besides, why would someone want to be alone with an impostor when the real you is someone so special? Review what you wrote. How much of it is something you created? How much of it is someone else's fault? Is there anything that you could have done to change your childhood past? There is a very strong chance that the answer to that question is 'No.' This is the time that you apply my version of the serenity prayer:

God, grant me the serenity to accept the things I cannot change,

The courage to change the things I can,

And the wisdom to know the difference.

Living one day at a time;

Enjoying one moment at a time;

Accepting hardship as the pathway to peace.

God is in control of this sinful world as it is,

The world is not as I would have it.

I know that God will make everything alright,

If I surrender to His Will,

That I may be reasonably happy in this life,

And supremely happy with Him.

Examining everything you wrote explains why you perceive life the way you do. That's the reason God wanted time alone with you. His goal is to remind you of why He created you to begin with.

If you had a loving childhood, be thankful for what you probably took for granted. If your childhood was filled with abuse and neglect, you of all people possess the ability to understand the value of being loved. No one better than you understands the importance of loving or hurting people. Jesus said, 'As you have done to one of these little ones, have you also done unto me.' Christian or not, that was God's way of telling us that we are all His children and we need to love one another. True love starts with loving yourself. The only person you can fix is yourself.

Your goal is to change the content of your world and

that begins with changing what's in your heart. From this day forward, speak only on the things that you can do something about. Anything else is a waste of time. Take control of your thoughts. Thoughts become things.

In the beginning God spoke things into existence. Everything He declared happened. Before He saw it, He spoke it. I have a question for you: Whose image are you created in? You are created in God's image. Therefore, whatever you speak, you will have. Allow your heart to be filled with hope, joy, faith and love. Out of the abundance of your heart your mouth will speak. In other words, what's in your heart will come out your mouth. Create some new self-fulfilling prophecies. If you think negatively, then negativity is what you will draw to yourself.

The history on those sheets of paper is your template. It represents all that is right and wrong about your perceptions of life. Some of it is derived from other people, some of it came from your environment, but at some point, it is obvious that your perceptions were reinforced by you. The first part of your life is a biography (written by someone else), but part two is an autobiography (it's what you write about yourself). Perceptions are equal to a chart; used properly, it can work as a road map helping you understand why you think, say and do things the way you do.

It is time for you to change your perceptions. When you were a child, you thought as a child, now you are an adult. It is time to put away childish things. During your youth you were given a map created by other people but times have changed and that map is growing out of date. You're given charge to navigate your life. This exercise revealed where you began and we're going to use that information to effectively guide you where you need to go. Only a fool follows an out-of-date map—especially one that they know leads nowhere. Now's the time to put yourself on course.

REVIEWING YOUR CHILDHOOD

Let's start with the first section on your early childhood. How you were treated between ages three and seven has a direct correlation to what your inner child needs. In every king there is a little boy; in every queen, a little girl. Whatever that baby didn't get as a child is still missing. In some cases it's hugs, in others it should have been a spanking. It is up to you to give your inner child the nurturing or discipline it needs. Subconsciously you will either attempt to recreate what provided you security or bring balance to what you didn't get as a child to your current environment. Keep in mind that this is based on what you experienced during that stage of your life and at some point you must accept the status quo. You cannot unstrike a match; however, you can learn not to play with fire. Some people experience such turmoil in life because they simply can't let go and move forward. If that is you, it's okay to get professional help. Find a good life coach, clergy or therapist. Make sure they are a good fit and can relate to you culturally. What I mean by this is to choose a professional who understands where you're coming from.

Race, age and gender have nothing do with wisdom and compassion.

This is a good time to examine something I strongly agree with, and that is 'Maslow's Hierarchy of Needs.' After we meet the physiological needs (breathing, thirst, hunger, sleep, sex) we are more capable of dealing with life's issues. I am going to provide a list that identifies some of Maslow's categories. His theory suggests that a person cannot grow to the next level until the previous one is satisfied. I know that to be true based on both personal and professional experience.

The needs are listed in order of development:

- Security—physical safety, freedom from threats etc.

- Social Needs—belonging, affection, interacting with people

- Psychological Safety Needs— Self-esteem, reputation, status

- Fulfillment and Self Actualization

Keep the list in mind as you explore your mini-autobiography. It may explain why your caregivers (and even yourself) function as they do. How can you feel relaxed when you're worried about putting food on the table? How can you make love if you feel that your safety is at risk? How can you experience fulfillment if you're worried about your reputation? Keep this in mind as you judge yourself and your caregivers. Now back to your life's saga.

During ages nine to fifteen you begin to confirm or reject the deposit that others contributed to your life. Take a moment and consider some correlations. When you are supported, embraced, and rewarded for your efforts, don't you thrive? Especially at anything that gives you validation. What is your source of validation as an adult? Ask yourself if this behavior could be associated with things that happened in your youth. It is not surprising that young men are prone to gangs and violence or girls are prone to promiscuity when belongingness needs go unmet. In adults, lack of validation causes loneliness.

Loneliness is a strong feeling of emptiness, isolation and solitude. Loneliness is often compared to feeling unwanted and unimportant. Human beings have a belongingness need. If rejection occurs in adolescence, chances are you will internalize your stress and attempt to compensate for it in adulthood. Addiction, depression, and inability to control anger are the fruits of lost faith, and hope. If you find yourself shopping too much, overeating, chain smoking, having unsuccessful relationships it is because you have either learned it from modeling or it is a coping mechanism for your broken places. You're using those coping mechanisms to deal with feelings of loneliness. If you don't acknowledge this problem many other dependent personality disorders will surface. There is a cure for loneliness. Go back a reread the last chapter. If you do what it says, I promise you will not have the void that creates loneliness.

Knowing why you have certain predispositions is key to

your ability to avoid being victimized by them. Nothing works better in taking the first step toward ending loneliness than admitting you're lonely, hurting and then having a good cry. Anything you repress or suppress will project itself in an unhealthy way. Typically things, people, places and sex are the outlet. Sex, people and things cannot fill a void that only you and God can satisfy. It is important that in this season you become complete being by yourself. The ability to be by yourself is a sign of maturity and growth.

It is the time to distinguish between lonely, loneliness and alone. Alone is a good thing. The definition of 'lonely' is sad because one has no friends or company. You are not lonely, because you have yourself and God. For a person to grow one must experience 'solitude.' Solitude is the state of being alone and secluded from other people, and often implies having made a conscious choice to be alone. Wisdom and maturity come from solitude.

You are a very complex being. Getting acquainted with yourself is a key factor in someone else getting to know you. If you can't be alone with yourself, what in the hell makes you think someone else wants to be? Your ability to convey feelings, express thoughts and impart experiences to others is pivotal in forming healthy relationships. Intimacy is just like it sounds, in-to-me-see. Transparency is an attractive quality. The beauty of life is that nobody is perfect. Our flaws are like the grooves of a key. They fashion us to fit with certain people. Not everyone is going to like you. Thank God for that. That in itself gives value to the people who love and accept you for who and what you are.

Experiences in life conjure up repressed feelings. The way your life starts is orchestrated by events you are subjected to over which you have no control. You don't have a say in whether you're born a bastard child, like me, or if you are conceived by two people who planned your conception. The choice of wealth or poverty is outside your grasp. As a matter of fact, you have no say if your parent or parents are genius or dummies. But the good news is that you made it here alive. You are here for a reason and you definitely matter.

Let me throw a bit of science into this. Your mother was born with millions of eggs in her ovaries. And millions of sperm pass via your father's loins. Do the math. It is no accident with odds like that stacked against you, that you made it here for a reason. Let's move on to the next chapter and find out what that is!

CHAPTER 6

BETTER, NOT BITTER

TURNING A CURSE INTO A BLESSING

Breaking up is a process, not an event. In reality, people surviving life traumas such as war, natural disasters, or the death of a loved one, don't just get over it. The same is true for breakups. Whether it simply ran its course, was a mistake to start with, or involved domestic abuse or infidelity, ending a relationship is tough. Why your relationship ended doesn't matter. Breaking up, like any other traumatic situation, has taxing effects long after it's over. Equip yourself to handle:

- ◆ Good and bad days
- ◆ Feeling like a failure due to a failed relationship
- ◆ Feeling like a loser, mixed with disappointment

- Suffering from separation anxiety
- Feelings of detachment
- Denial—acting as if nothing is bothering you (can't heal that way)
- An ongoing battle with guilt trips

Whatever the case, be it that you just cared about someone, or really loved them, ending a relationship will do one of two things. It will make you bitter, or better.

Separation anxiety causes you to experience debilitating symptoms. It's not uncommon to wake up in the middle of the night with your heart pounding or a nightmare. Sometimes in the middle of the day, out of nowhere, you could find yourself barely able to catch your breath or unable to remain focused. At other times you feel as though you're watching someone else's life, and you have lost interest in things that typically bring you joy.

If these things are happening to you, it's normal. You may be suffering anxiety due to the stress of the breakup, separation or divorce. Know that you're not alone. Using war as an example, one would think that after enduring life and death circumstances on a daily basis, healing from traumatic wounds, and returning home, a person would be glad that the nightmare was finally over. Some people can't understand why soldiers aren't able to just get on with life. Yeah right. If you're normal, if you are a human being, you have feelings. All the prayer, self-help books, and cocktails in the world can't instantly heal a broken heart or make a guilt trip go away. Love, like war, can be hell.

This chapter will teach you how to navigate past anxiety, stress and bitterness. What was meant to curse you will bless you. I am going to coach you how to use this experience to make you 'Better' not 'Bitter.' As a child, every time I was about to get a whipping, Dad would tell me, 'This is going to hurt me more than it does you.' I remember thinking, 'Right, then let me whip you.' My point is that some things are easier said than done. Life is filled with challenges and trials that you must endure alone. Every decision made comes with consequences. Sometimes you are reaping what you've sown; other times, God is removing someone from your life that you don't want gone. It could be that you're ending a relationship that never should have begun. Your Spirit knows what is best for you when you don't. Ending an ill-suited relationship hurts as much as breaking off a destructive one. Remember, this is a process.

The first thing I want you to learn is: you are much stronger than you think. Weeping may endure for a night, but joy is coming in the morning. It may not be this morning, but I assure you it is coming.

Here are signs that indicate you're cycling from normal to anxiety mode. Are any of these statements familiar?

- 'I can't stop thinking about this...'
- 'I can't sleep.'
- 'I can't concentrate.'
- 'Had I followed my first mind...'
- 'I should have...'

- 'I don't feel like doing anything.'
- 'If I hadn't...'
- 'I could have...'
- 'I don't have an appetite.'

If you find yourself making any of those statements on a routine basis you're still in the recovery stage. Nonetheless, it's time to stop it! Focus on things you can actually do something about. You cannot go back in time. God answered your prayers by moving you forward. You may not like the answer, but He knows what you need, when you need it and how to give it you. Every moment spent focusing on things that you can't do a damn thing about is a waste of time. Time that you will not get back.

You finally made the right decision by ending this fiasco so stop regretting it. You did the right thing. Many of us spend so much time in an unbalanced state, we've forgotten what being calm and relaxed feels like. Now it's time to do what is best for everyone, especially yourself. That is a heck of a lot easier said than done. It is only natural to question yourself and do the 'what ifs.' Who do you know that likes failing at anything?

Nobody likes losing. Losing doesn't mean that you're a loser. Doing the right thing is one thing, working through the process is another. It's the equivalent of finding out you need surgery. Being diagnosed is one thing, but getting admitted to the hospital and undergoing surgery is another. However, if you want to live you must complete the procedure and go through the healing process. What you are doing right now is comparable to an emotional-mental surgical procedure.

Experiencing separation anxiety after a break up is normal. Anxiety and depression cycles are going to happen, no matter why your relationship ended. It could be that someone kicked you to the curb and you did nothing to deserve it. Perhaps you got booted because you kept taking someone for granted or mistreated them, let them go. You had your chance. Stop being selfish and allow that person to be happy. Whatever the case, let it go and trust God. Download T.D. Jakes' 'Let it Go' and read it daily until you know it by heart.

At this stage, you're finally coming to grips with the fact that your relationship is over. Now let's get on with the process of healing. The difference between being cured and healed is simple. When you're cured, there is a scar or some sign that you were once afflicted. However, when you are healed, there are no scars. There is little, if any, evidence that you were ever afflicted. By the end of this chapter, you will be well on your way to being fully healed. This season of your life will have made you a better, much wiser person.

STRESS AND ITS EFFECTS

Let's examine the effects of stress. It is not uncommon for children to regress when they suffer trauma, especially separation from a loved one. Toddlers go back to sippie cups, wetting themselves and having night terrors. Older kids become clingy and accident-prone. Teenagers and young adults engage in risky behavior, develop physical symptoms, become easily irritable, or sleep a great deal. As an adult you must accept that you are human too. The child inside you is wounded. It is up to you to be mature enough to realize that a breakup is a process, and it is going to take time for you to heal. There will be good and bad days for all involved, but you must persevere. Nothing is wrong with crying. Jesus wept! The one thing you cannot do is go backwards. This relationship ended for a reason. It ended for the good of all concerned.

Though it's hard, it is time to gain control over your thought process. Only a fool continues to do the same thing expecting a different outcome. You must do some things for yourself. 'Never send a changing individual to an unchanging environment,' just as taking a bath, then putting on dirty socks, underwear and clothes defeats the purpose of bathing. Cleaning your emotions up and then returning to the source of your pain is foolish. Realize when you feel stressed and remove yourself from the source.

If you want to succeed at healing, here are some rules that you cannot break:

- You cannot go backwards.
- Don't put new wine in an old skin.
- Remember: You may have changed but that does not mean everyone else did too.
- Be an individual and an independent thinker.
- Remember, you aren't alone. You have yourself and God.

Having difficulty in regulating your feelings is normal. Preoccupation with either revenge against, or allegiance with, your ex is human nature. Nonetheless, I am warning you that not managing those emotions is dangerous. Allowing yourself to play with fire will result in your getting burned.

You may feel temporary satisfaction from talking to, seeing or being around the person who God removed from your life, but you will regret it. There is a reason your spirit and God removed you from that situation to start with. Better to leave well enough alone or here is what is going to happen: First, temporarily, you are going to forget the previous trauma caused by the failed relationship. Feelings of detachment or sexual depersonalization (that means having sex based on the moment and familiarity) i.e. every reason, but the right ones) will come next. Simultaneously, you wind up experiencing shame, guilt, and become riddled with persistent feelings of helplessness. Following that, you will experience a loss of value for the things that give your life meaning such as a family, spiritual faith, hope and the ability to trust others. In the end, despair will take over. The longer you engage with your ex, the more passive-aggressive behavior will develop, which can result in depressive, anxious or even suicidal thoughts. By the time you reach 'the end' again, you are going to feel unhappy, frustrated, heavy-hearted and maybe even explosively angry. To avoid this, leave well enough alone. Quit while you are ahead. That relationship ended for a reason—your own good!

Sleep problems, trouble concentrating, hyper-vigilance to threats (being paranoid that everyone is going to dog you out), and irritability are not good for you. They are co-morbid signs of anxiety, stress and separation. Adding to this problem is the fact that those feelings are contagious. Nonetheless, you cannot give in to those feelings. Suppose something good did come your way, how could it benefit you if you allow those destructive thoughts to overcome you? If you aren't careful you will run your blessing off.

You have the right to be walking around emotionally traumatized, but you owe it to yourself not to let the weaker part of your being win. You are much stronger than you think. If the going gets tough remember what's going on inside you affects everyone and everything you touch. If you have children or work in a profession that affects the lives and safety of other people, or have to function at a clear, mental and emotional level, you need to be at your best. Life can be unfair, but you can do all things through God that strengthens you. Greater is that which is in you than any problem you have in this world. Speak blessing over yourself. Encourage yourself!

Out of the abundance of your heart, your mouth will speak. Stress and heartache cause you to be ill-focused and short with those you need most. It's no secret that on a bad day most people aren't at their best so just remember, 'You can do all things through God that strengthens you.' Greater is He that is in you, than all the negative and evil things in this world. Hint: A little rest and prayer go a long way. Even Jesus slept.

Research has shown people who suffered posttraumatic stress disorders have a smaller hippocampus than those that haven't been exposed to trauma. I am mentioning this for a reason. The hippocampus is the part of the brain the controls memory. Your body corrects things on the inside, but it's your responsibility to fix your external environment. Studies show that prolonged stress causes the hippocampus to shrink, thus inhibiting your ability to remember and limiting the potential to create new memories. It's up to you to focus on the future and not the past. If your emotions are accompanied by physical sensations, take a break.

Failing doesn't make you a failure. Learning from a mistake turns a mistake into a lesson. Used properly, that lesson converts to a blessing. The trick is to stop exposing yourself to the source of your problem. No matter how tempting, you cannot keep exposing yourself to your ex or anything connected to them. This is a season where your focus needs to be on you. If you can't handle being alone with yourself, who else would want to? You can do several things to become 'better' at being alone with yourself. Here are a few tips:

<u>Learn how to chill out.</u> Practice techniques that strengthen your ability to relax. Solitary activities enrich the soul. Prayer, meditation, and self- actualization are best done alone. If you find yourself having a panic attack use controlled breathing; it will aid you in becoming less reactive and make you less vulnerable to anxiety and stress. Also, focus on goals that you have put off achieving. You

have plenty to do that doesn't involve being dependent on someone else.

Get a life. Instead of self-medicating with prescription pills, a glass of wine, sex, or a joint, get out, get some exercise, start a hobby or go back to school. Get involved in your church or community and develop good relationships with friends and family members who have character, integrity, good morals, and common sense. An idle mind is the devil's playground.

Arrest negative thoughts. Put stupidity on probation. Pick a time to deal with problems. Set aside a day and limited amount of time to deal with your mental dirt. Accept the things that you have no control over and let them go. If you're going to have a pity party, at least schedule it.

Anxiety is a physiological problem. Relationships involve use of your mind, body and soul. The id, ego and super ego, all of your being, must be engaged if you are to find mental, physiological and emotional equilibrium. Use every part of yourself to take victory over stress and anxiety. The body and mind are very much connected and I will suggest a few things you can do to connect your physical senses with emotional states. Love, peace and joy are co-dependent.

TECHNIQUES TO TRANSFORM YOUR DAY

Use the following techniques to transform a bland day to a beautiful one. The fantastic part is everything that's on my list you can do alone and with little, or no, money. Gender, age and race have nothing to do with utilizing these techniques. They work for everyone.

The eyes are the key to the soul. There are two types of vision: mental and physical. The end objective is to enjoy a beautiful view. It can start with something as simple remembering beautiful moments in your life and writing them down. Treasured photos, new and old, are wonderful for bringing a smile to your face. Nature affords us magnificent views for free. Sunsets, sunrises, parks, lakes, mountains and beaches are there for the taking. Make time to notice the simple things in your immediate environment. Start with the architecture, flowers, trees, little kids playing etc.

Tasting things is a simple source of pleasure. I didn't say eat a whole cake, pizza or gallon of ice cream. I am referring to simple things like a good piece of fruit, hot tea or coffee, or a good healthy meal. Done right, those things always bring a smile to your face. The trick is taking the time to enjoy it. Don't wolf down your food like it's your last meal. Savor the flavor.

Touch is a wonderful sense. Enjoy a long steamy hot shower or soaking in a hot bath; nothing is more soothing. Put on a comfortable set of PJs, you know, the kind that feel good next to your skin. Wrap up in your favorite blanket, 300+ count sheets and a good pillow. If you can't afford a new mattress, get some memory foam or egg crate foam for your bed. It works wonders and you will love the way it feels. Invest in a new set of sleeping pillows. They are well worth the money. Try giving or getting a massage, petting your cat, dog, horse or gorilla (okay you may not want to pet a gorilla). Bottom line, contact is a sense that we take for granted, but it is what makes us most human.

It is no secret that fragrances can soothe. Taking the time to smell the roses is more than just a figure of speech. Fresh flowers and plants brighten a room. You would be surprised how much the scent of vanilla, mint or cinnamon can change the environment. Nothing beats the smell of an ocean breeze. Baby powder, lavender, baked goods or even scented candles are proven to change mood and attitudes for the better. Open some windows and let fresh air in your house. If you are still smoking, designate a room for it and buy an air filtration device for that room (or better yet, stop smoking - it causes more stress than it ever relieves).

Last, but not least, is hearing. Silence is more than golden, it's priceless. The beauty of hearing is that it works on both ends of the spectrum. Quiet, peaceful environments allow you to get in touch with your inner self. We are so bombarded by sound, more than often we freak out when it's quiet. On the other hand, the sounds of nature, a bubbling brook, ocean waves, birds chirping or the wind blowing are naturally soothing. Listening to soft, inspirational, or classical music has been shown to lower blood pressure and reduce stress.

The psychological aspect of anxiety is not as difficult to deal with as you may think. Knowing what to do and how to do it is the key to controlling stress and stress-filled situations. If you're seeing a therapist, doing what's on this list may greatly reduce the need to do so. Knowledge gives you power. Many of my colleagues won't like me for this, but you are capable of treating yourself. The trick is knowing what triggers your anxiety and doing something about it right then. Your mind is the source of your negative thought processes; it also houses solutions for the issues that cause you repetitive stress. You may not be able to change the person, place or situation, but you do have control over how those things affect you.

WAYS TO REDUCE STRESS

The following are ways you can reduce or eliminate those stressful moments. It's all about controlling your response to those moments. Whenever you find yourself tripping, thinking about, or living in, the past use these techniques to rid yourself of such problems:

Take advantage of the fact you're not a beast. Human beings possess the ability to calm themselves down. Thinking before you act proves that you're not immature, out of control, or just plain stupid. That in itself forces people to respect you. Runaway stress overwhelms the body and mind. It interferes with your ability to outwit circumstances and people. Another way to think of this is, act the same way you would if you were in front of the police. Because if you don't, there is a strong possibility that you will be. You are able to control yourself. It's up to you to choose to do so!

Learn and use nonverbal communication skills. Non-verbal communication consists of:

- Eye Contact—don't stare someone down, or avoid looking at them.

- Facial Expression—smile before you start talking (even if you don't want to). Tense looks create bad vibes.

- Tone of Voice—Keep your tone lower than theirs; never be aggressive.

- Posture and Gesture—Avoid folded arms, clenched fists or turning your back.

- Touch—Be gentle, make slow deliberate movements.

- Timing and Pace—Don't be in a hurry, speak calmly and slowly.

Watch how you stand. Get in the habit of standing at least 12 to 18 inches away from people when you talk to them. Nobody likes to have their personal space invaded. Deliberately speak in a soft tone. A soft tongue turns away wrath. It is better to deliver a message rather than invoke one. Engagement is the antithesis of control. Your goal is to communicate, not win, in a conversation. Practice challenging conversations in the mirror, or using a recorder or with a friend. Doing this prior to attempting them in person will spare you a great deal of unnecessary confrontation. Being ghetto, talking with your neck, head, and hands is not only offensive, it makes you look ignorant as hell. If you cannot control yourself, put your hands in your pocket, hold a beverage in your hand, or find a place to put both your hands. I suggest folding them across the mid section just above your naval. Never point or fold your arms when talking about a tense subject. Bottom line, you don't want to be intimidating; no one likes to be provoked.

<u>Don't take everything so seriously.</u> You can do this and still demonstrate to others that you value what concerns them. Humor and lightheartedness is beneficial when it comes to dealing with problems. Playful communication can reduce tension during stressful, anxious times. This technique elevates mood, lowers your blood pressure and stress levels. Things that might be difficult to express can be easier said when you use gentle humor. Attempt to be creative when you discuss a difficult subject.

<u>Stay focused on your conversation.</u> It is much easier to handle one subject than three. If your goal is to resolve old hurts and resentments, handle your current problem tactfully. Timing is everything. Don't attempt to discuss anything when you or the other person is having a bad day. A simple way to do that is ask, 'Is this a good time to talk?' If the person says no, then don't. If they say yes, do not make matters worse by saying things like, 'You aren't going to like this,' 'This is probably going to upset you,' 'I know you don't want to be bothered with this.' Get to the point, speak softly, say what you have to say. Allow the person time to think and react. If they don't want to talk then, respect and accept that. Above all, before you do or say anything, put yourself in the other person's shoes. Do unto others as you would have them do unto you.

<u>End conflicts that cannot be resolved.</u> It takes two people to argue. You or the other person has the right to disengage at any time. Accept that you may never agree.

Finally, our goal is to be 'Better, not Bitter.' Moving forward is a wonderful thing. The lesson known is where you've been; the greater unknown is where God is taking you. It is your destiny. Getting to the next level is 100% preparation. Success is preparation meeting opportunity. What you think and do today will create your tomorrow. This is your check list. After completing it you are ready to proceed to the next level. Some of the activities will be ongoing. Remember this is a process.

TEN STEPS TOWARD YOUR FUTURE

Realize that this process is normal. It's about the journey, not the destination. Your goal is to complete each phase, not rush to the next one.

You control mourning time. Pity parties are okay, as long as you give them a start and end time. Don't wear out your welcome.

Control your thought process. Don't have panic attacks, attack your panic. Tell your mind what to think, not the other way around. Your mind is a movie theater, and you're the owner. You show what you want, when you want.

Every day, do something for one of your senses. Engage all of you. Sometimes give your eyes a treat, next day let your ears be the center of attention, and so on...

Start a blessing diary. Every day write down something good that happened, no matter how small. If you are faithful over the little blessings, God will send the big ones your way.

Communicate with the positive people in your life at least once every three days. Not only do the appreciate it, you will too. Don't take good folk for granted. Friendship is a gift.

Everyday do something thoughtful for two people. One of these people is you. It can be as simple as holding a door open, paying someone a sincere compliment or saying good morning.

Pay attention to your emotions. If you are having a bad day, do something about it immediately. Pray, read an inspirational book like this one, call a friend that you can confide in. Take a different way home. Re-center yourself.

Be patient. As long as you breathe you are going to have good days and bad days. The goal is, at the end of the week, make sure that you take back the moments life stole from you.

View your frustrations and disappointments from new perspectives. How you perceive an issue will greatly affect your approach to it and its outcome.

You are in control of your destiny. Greater is He that is in you than He that is in the world. Don't you love yourself? Go ahead, give yourself a hug and a pat on the back. You're well on your way. Joy comes in the morning!

CHAPTER 7

JOY COMES IN THE MORNING

PREPARING FOR THE REST OF YOUR LIFE

What a big difference a day makes. Okay, I must admit, it's been more than a day. It's your moment, time to start anew. Previously, I stated, 'Weeping may endure for a night, but joy comes in the morning.' Our goal is ensuring that you don't blow the rest of the day. One of my favorite sayings is, 'Yesterday is history; tomorrow is a mystery; Right now is a 'gift,' that's why we call it the 'present.' If success is to be obtained in life, it will be directly related to what we do with this gift. I am referring to the gift of the 'present.'

The things you do from this moment forward will affect the rest of your life. It's time to stop keeping up appearances and get organized. You will either benefit from the goals you set today or suffer because you allowed your fears to stop you. Now's the time to gain control over your mind, remove irrational behaviors, and live, not just survive, the rest of your life. Let's give the real you what it's been asking for—a joy-filled life. We know the cost, now it's time to begin the journey.

You have many complicated decisions to make and so little time to make them. The question is, where do you go from here? This is the first day of the rest of your life. Do you know what to do with it? This chapter is dedicated to getting you to the next moment.

Until now, life has been about everything, and everybody, but you. At the beginning of this book the focus was on getting past a break up. The guilt trips, kids and stress were the primary concerns. As of today, you're not lonely anymore. Though this is a process you're well on your way to being Better and not Bitter. We are putting an end to keeping up appearances. It's time to return to being the person God created you to be. This is your season. Everything you do from today forward will bring transformation to every aspect of your life! If nothing else has been accomplished you have learned life is about living, not merely surviving. God created you to have life, and life more abundantly. Starting now, that is exactly what we are going to do!

Some people exist day by day and that's fine for them, but not for you. Those people are more concerned with how things appear, rather than how they are. Life is about quality. Knowing the price of everything but the value of nothing is for fools. You may be a lot of things but a fool isn't one. Who God created you to be is far better than who others say you are. It's sad that most of us are busy being byproducts of our imagination. Living in a vision is one thing; living out an illusion is another. Wouldn't you say it's about time to disconnect from the matrix?

Life is a series of moments connected by time. It is filled with ups and downs, failures and successes. What you do with these moments creates either success or failure. Your goal is to maximize the series of opportunities, also known as moments. Success is the result of you being the best you possible. This chapter gives you the tools to organize your life. It's time to become that which you were predestined to be. Impersonating yourself gets old. Being accountable one minute and irresponsible the next is a complete turn off, not to mention a major contribution to failure.

Achieving any goal requires that you remain self-motivated and focused. That is another thing that's easier said than done. A lack of motivation is the first step toward failure. It's time to get excited about creating success in your life. If you don't, who else will be? This may come as a shock to you, but most people could care less if you live or drop dead. If you don't believe me try this with a friend. Tell them, '_____' (celebrity) is dead. More than likely the next thing they will say is, 'Really, that's too bad.' Then the conversation will return to some subject concerning them or what they're doing. If you don't believe me, put the book down for a second and try it.........Told you.........(LOL). This is a season that you need to focus on you. Nobody can love you like you do. Back to this self-motivation thing.

There are three primary reasons you lose motivation.

- Lack of Faith in Yourself
- Lack of Focus
- Fear

Lack of faith in yourself is the number one reason people fail at achieving goals. You must positively reinforce yourself, because nobody else will do it for you. When you feel yourself losing momentum, look to your role models and mentors. Surround yourself with people who are aspiring to succeed at something, too. Though this is a solo journey, you are not alone. Use your support system. Allow your children, friends and family members in and let them be aware that you need some emotional support. It's important to encourage one another. Anything that someone else has achieved you can do, too. Your version may be different but you can do all things through God, Who strengthens you.

Successful people are human too. They made mistakes along the way and at one point in life they were where you are. Kobe and Lebron were kids at middle school basketball practice; they missed many shots and free throws, and often fouled out, but they didn't quit. Your doctor was a student; he had classes he hated, struggled with and probably was teased for being a nerd. Your hairstylist didn't always have it going on; the clients were dolls, relatives and friends, and the first shop was the living room. In other words you have to start somewhere. Be successful right where you are. Success comes from mastering the moment. Take no thought for tomorrow; tomorrow will take care of itself. Handle the business at hand; tomorrow will be here before you know it. Keep telling yourself, 'I can do anything I set my mind to.' Focus on succeeding at what you're doing right now.

The biggest detriment to focus is a lack of motivation. See yourself succeeding at your goal. Live the vision. Take control of your mind. Define your goals. And, every day, take at least three steps related to your plan. If you only accomplish three a day, at the end of the month you will have accomplished ninety things. If you do that, there is no way in hell that you can fail at anything. To encourage yourself, maintain a journal on what you have accomplished. Success breeds success, and keeping records of the little things reinforces your self-esteem.

How do you eat an elephant? One bite at a time. Intention matched with commitment yields success. Don't focus on what went wrong or what you couldn't get done. That leads to depression and procrastination. People lose focus when they pay attention to their setbacks more than their setups. Every time you achieve the smallest of steps, write it down. That will prove to you that you are more capable than you think. See the vision, write it down and make it plain. It's normal the feel lost sometimes but don't let fear kick in.

Fear is **F**alse **E**vidence **A**ppearing **R**eal. Over 95% of your fears will never happen. The 5% that's left, you don't see coming and there is not a damn thing you can do about it. Many people waste valuable time by sitting up wondering what might happen. Concern yourself with what you can make happen. Much of what you fear comes from focusing on past failures and being idle.

A self-fulfilling prophecy is something that you preconceive and through your actions make happen. There are two types: Positive and negative. An example of this is preparing for a test. If you say, 'This test is going to be hard as hell, there is no way I can pass,' then chances are you won't even bother putting forth your best effort and you'll flunk. Instead, use fear as a tool and create a strategy to attack your fear head on. If you think the test is hard, and you study hard, you will pass the most difficult exam. The difference between a positive and negative self-fulfilling prophecy is that the positive one is accompanied by effort. The negative one is accompanied by negativity, fear and doing nothing. Thoughts become things. Think positively and you will yourself to have positive results. Most of your fears are based on previous failures, negative thoughts, and discouraging comments from other people.

Hear are a few irrational fears:

- ◆ Making a mistake
- ◆ Feeling stupid
- ◆ Failure
- ◆ Change

- ◆ Authority
- ◆ Loneliness

I will address all of those irrational fears in a couple of paragraphs.

During your life you are going to make mistakes. The key is admitting and not repeating them. That's how you learn. Mistakes point out what you need to work on. They are not setbacks, but setups. Mistakes set you up to perfect your goals. Feeling stupid happens when you don't study your craft. The definition of stupid is lacking intelligence or common sense. Education fixes that. Surround yourself with good mentors and people who support your vision. Remain in a thriving environment and, if that means you need to relocate, move! Imitate successful people.

Surround yourself with successful people. What they do will serve as a template. Allow their good habits to rub off on you. Failure only takes place when you quit. If you don't give up, you can't fail. Use other peoples' criticism and doubt to inspire you. Change is part of growth so don't be upset when you must stop doing things your way. Life is about evolution. If something doesn't change or move, it becomes stagnant. Growth requires transformation.

Picture this: a caterpillar emerging from a cocoon but still walking everywhere it goes. You might say that's the dumbest butterfly you've ever seen. When you transform your life, you must leave the familiar. If you're transformed, make your actions reflect it. You can't do what you used to do or go where you used to go. Live the dream.

Take authority over your life. Productive environments are governed by authority. You have jurisdiction over your life; nonetheless, you must be accountable. Even self-employed people are accountable to their clients. The more discipline you have, the more successful you will be.

Busy people aren't lonely. Get off your butt and stay on task. Set a day-to-day strategy. Measure where you are in relation to your goals. Engage recurrent fears with combative strategies. You are the master of your fate, the captain of your soul. Greater is He that is in you, than anything you face in this world. The God that began a good and perfect work in you will see it through to its perfection. Remember, faith without works is dead. Life's race does not go to the swift, nor the strong, but to those who endure. Hang in there, you can do this!

What you believe will happen, is going to happen. This is especially true when your vision is supported by actions. Focusing on what you don't have, on what you want, puts you on the pathway toward defeat. Instead, focus on your next step and what you have to work with. Pay attention to positive things in your life. Appreciate all that is right. Success is a direct result of a good attitude and deliberate actions applied to goals. Another way to put this is, get organized. Preparation meeting opportunity is success.

ACHIEVING YOUR GOALS

Declaring your intention is the first step toward success. People don't plan to fail, they fail to plan. Organization, strategy and preparation are the foundation for attainable goals. The key to achieving your goals is effective planning. By definition, a goal is the object of your ambition with a date attached to it. Another way to look at this is: A goal is your will, the precedent for what you want to achieve in life.

Perhaps you have set several goals in your past, only to have them dissolve or wind up on the shelf. This time that is not going to happen. We are going to eliminate the fantasy factor. Instead it will be replaced with a sound, tangible and realistic strategy. This time if you don't succeed, it won't be because you didn't have the tools to work with. Your failure will be because you weren't serious about transforming your life to begin with. To whom much is given, much is required. Achieving worthwhile aspirations involves commitment and hard work.

If a person gives you a gift, that's one thing. When God gives you a present, that is yet another. Time is the one thing that you cannot create. Money can't buy it. Waste it if you want, but you'll never get it back. There are only twenty-four hours in a day. You sleep for eight, work eight, and maybe commute for one. That leaves you seven hours for yourself, family, fun, goals, shopping, eating and friends. Obviously, it would be foolish to waste any time you have left. Maximizing moments is directly related to getting the most out of your life.

I suggest that you sit and write down how you typically use your time over a week. Be honest. Chances are you waste a great deal of it. How often are you late? How much time do you waste talking about things you need to be doing? If you don't examine how effective you are, how can you become more productive?

Let's begin by creating time management goals. Step one, controlling what you do with your schedule, is paramount. The objective is to change your behavior in order to attain whatever goal you set for yourself. Take this week to eliminate non-productive activities. It could be something as simple as limiting your time on the Internet or making time for yourself to read. Start leaving twenty minutes early for a meeting, going to work and social events. When you are on time, you will have far less stress and people will notice the change immediately. Being late is rude and trifling. If you don't respect your time, how can you respect others?

Use time management tools. Day planners, software programs, even your cell phone, can help you be more productive. Give yourself fifteen minutes for non-crucial activities in order to stop yourself from wasting time. People respect you more when you value their time; otherwise it demonstrates of lack of professionalism and focus. And if people are late and don't value your time, leave after waiting fifteen minutes. They will take you far more seriously next time. There is no need to be rude, your actions speak louder than words. If you are going to be late, call at least an hour ahead of time and tell the other party you need to reschedule for another day.

If you are a business owner, delegate tasks. Outsourcing

needed deliverables will aid in your productivity. Get in the habit of limiting activities. Don't spend more than fifteen minutes on the phone unless absolutely necessary. Try not to spend more than twenty minutes on writing and reading emails. Before starting a meeting, inform the person you're meeting with that you have to leave at a certain time. Your meeting will be far more productive.

Life is precious. You owe it to yourself to get the most out of your life. Work time, play time and family time should be just that. Mixing them up robs you of productivity and enjoyment. If you don't manage those properly, you will never have any 'me' time. Believe me, you need time to and for yourself. Imagine that you are on a flight and the cabin loses pressure. What does the steward say about the oxygen mask? 'Put yours on first, then help the person next to you.' You can't be of use to someone else when you haven't taken proper care of yourself. Without proper rest you are no good to anybody. When fatigued, you're sluggish, easily irritated, and running behind yourself. If you are hurried, you are a pain in the butt to yourself and everyone else. Take the time, daily, to add up how much time you waste. You cannot achieve goals without managing time.

Setting goals is a process. Ask yourself what is the first thing that you need to do to get your life in order. Realistic goals aren't grandiose. Achieving small manageable desires can transform your life. Start with constructive objectives because worthy goals empower you. Legitimate goals contribute to your independence. They stabilize life and create opportunities for growth. This is a very critical season in your life so be sure of what you want. Seven to twelve years from now, you are going to either benefit, or be cursed by, what you do today. Do not just throw something out there: think. Take a good look at how you're living. Here some things to consider:

- Do you have a job?
- Do you need transportation?
- Do you have your own place?
- Do you have children you must provide for?
- Do you need to make lifestyle changes?
- Do you need to increase your earning potential?
- Do you need to make a career change?
- Do you need to reduce your expenses?

Identify one goal that you can achieve in thirty days or less. Commit to a time frame and choose a start date. Make sure that what you picked is necessary and worthwhile. Next select another goal that you can achieve in ninety days.

Here is a way to make sure you picked the right objective: Look at what you chose in reverse. Meaning, if you don't do it, what are the consequences six months to a year later? Will you wish you did it? Will you regret putting it off? The purpose of any goal is to eliminate stress, struggle and to move you ahead in life. If your goal doesn't have a positive, motivating quality, you are wasting your time. Don't bother with it, you will be upset in the end.

All worthwhile objectives require sacrifice. If your goal doesn't require you to give up something, it's not much of a goal. Anything worth doing takes effort and time. Commitment is key. Without dedication, I promise you won't succeed. Effort, hard work and sacrifice force success your way. If you take one step, God will take two.

Prayer, emotional support and encouragement are as good as money. Surround yourself with people who want to see you do better. Sometimes you are going to need help from people who have your interests at heart. Embrace those who support you but don't be surprised if so-called 'friends and family' aren't among your support system. Typically they don't join in until you prove yourself. You can pay them back when they want to borrow money.

Start out small and make each goal your number one priority. Often people fail because they take on too much to soon. An example is losing weight. Don't start off by saying you want to lose a hundred pounds in three months. Try losing five pounds every two weeks; it's far less stressful and more realistic. It may not seem like much; nonetheless, it's achievable. If you remain consistent and set workable goals, not only will you meet your objective, more than likely, you will exceed them. Tell the right people what you are doing. That will lock you in. Allow your haters to encourage you. Use their negativity to motivate you to succeed. There is no sweeter revenge than being successful.

Life comes with problems, so be prepared to alter your plans but no matter what, don't quit. Always be ready to adjust to circumstances. Be willing to persevere. Failure is not an option. Every time you stop, it takes that much longer to complete the task. When times get tough, put your ego and pride in the trash. Take the help. God will always have a ram in the bush for you. Consider it divine intervention because that is exactly what it is. God wants to see you succeed, He works through people. Sometimes He puts obstacles there to keep you humble or to teach the people around you what you're made of. In the end, you will celebrate with the people who were sent to help you along the way. It is no accident that they were there. FYI, I would never have made it, if so many wonderful people hadn't been there for me.

To position yourself for a successful future, rid yourself of negative, irrational behaviors. The spectrum of self-defeating human behavior has no limits. For your convenience I grouped them into five categories:

- Dealing with the past
- Overcoming limitations
- Embracing the new you
- Comparing yourself to other people
- Unreal expectations
- Controlling mental triggers

Now that it is morning, stop focusing on the hellish night, days, weeks and months that preceded it. You have officially made it through the storm. When someone throws your past and its failures in your face, and they will, ignore them. The only person you can control is yourself. Truthfully, you more than likely contributed to the opinion they had of the old you.

That was then, this is now and your job is to live in the present. The opinions of other people will catch up to you if you remain focused and stay on track. Unless you are acting like the old you, you have nothing to prove to anyone but yourself and God. Actions speak louder than words so remain focused and stay steadfast in pursuit of the new you.

No gift comes without struggle. This time around, manage your time properly. Now that you know what to do, 'Just do It.' The only limitations you have are what your mind can conceive. As long as you put works with your faith, success is yours. Succeeding at life is a process not an event. You are much stronger than you think and limitations are excuses. Excuses are tools that incompetent people use to justify failure.

You are getting closer to becoming the person God created you to be. Remember that character and integrity are the key constituents for success. Comparing yourself to anyone, including the old you is only beneficial for one thing—stress. Measure yourself against what you're capable of doing. You know yourself.

You are a unique individual and nobody can offer the world what you have to give it. That is why God created you. There is a reason for your existence and, as you fine-tune your gifts, your purpose will find you. The talents you possess will bring you before great men. Your gift will make room for you.

Having realistic expectations is the key to being successful. Rome wasn't built in a day, but it was destroyed in one. That occurred because someone knew how to pull the emperor's trigger. Every good or bad reaction happens in your life as a result of someone pulling your trigger. Statements, people, places, things, and situations trigger reactions in you. Learn what triggers you, then master those triggers to empower yourself.

CHAPTER 8

PRACTICE WHAT YOU PREACH

HOW TO FIND THE RIGHT PERSON FOR YOURSELF

Be that which you seek. Love is the only game two can play and, in this case, both parties lose. So, before you try to find love again, let's make sure you're ready. The first step is know the rules of the game. Leaving the cocoon is hard enough but after all the introspection you've done, ending up with the wrong person would be devastating. It's time to protect your investment in yourself.

Success in love comes from knowing who and what to avoid because love doesn't love just anyone. Becoming the person God created you to be is hard work. A big part of the equation is being that which you seek, but that in itself doesn't ensure success. Dealing with unfinished business, fine tuning your instincts, knowing the dating rules, your presentation, understanding body language, and having good timing is the other part. Let's get started.

Before meeting someone new, all your unfinished business with other people needs to be completed. How could you embrace your future holding on to the past? It's impossible to take steps forward and move backwards at the same time. If you're dealing with someone out of familiarity, holding onto guilt about a specific relationship, still bitter with an ex, or wondering 'What if' then you are not ready to date anyone. Clean out your emotional closet first. Starting a new relationship with 'baggage' will put unnecessary strain on what could be a potentially good thing. Being honest with yourself, and having good moral character and an attitude of openness is great. That's needed to create room in your life for someone new. But, intention without corresponding actions isn't going to take you far. If anything, you're stroking yourself. You have to let go of your past. If you don't, you are going to end up in a mess and more confused than before. Being intimate with people divides you. How can you be a whole person if you're cut in half?

Reaching out to ex-lovers for closure is never a good thing unless you truly have unfinished business. It is the equivalent of digging up a loved one and reliving the funeral. If something is dead, let it remain so. Absence doesn't make the heart grow fonder; if anything, it creates room for doubt and allows other people to enter your life.

Also it sets up a precedent that suggests you or your ex can go in and out of each other's life at will. Not only is that stupid, it's self-defeating. Life is too short and death is too long for such melodrama.

Instead, do some introspection. The answers to your needs are housed inside you, not in a dysfunctional relationship with another person. The person that you're obsessed with isn't thinking about you. That old relationship ended for a reason so leave well enough alone and move on with your life. This will prevent old attitudes and paranoia from migrating into a fresh situation. Some people hold on to dead relationships because they feel they are on a time limit. God created time. If you feel as though you're about the run out, ask Him for some more.

Hint: Stop wasting time chasing what's left of a dead situation! There are other ways to bring closure.

Writing a letter is a better option than talking to your ex in person or over the phone. I strongly suggest you consider taking that route. It will be far more productive by allowing you to say everything while purging yourself of accumulated stress. If that is not an option for you, here is how you handle your situation. Stay focused. Any meeting or conversation you have must be based on the issue at hand and nothing more. Be courteous and straightforward in your discussions. Remember, you're the one with the problem—not them. Keep to the agenda because this conversation is about clearing the air, not a reunion or a memorial.

Meeting in person has the potential to turn into something very ugly. But, if you're stupid enough to do it, do more listening than talking. You might learn something. Don't expect to come away proving some monumental point. At best, you will have gotten something off your chest. After doing this, ask yourself what you learned from the experience. Don't go back for seconds. The fact that you had to do such a thing indicates you are not through grieving, have ego issues and need more time to yourself. It's the equivalent of going to a gravesite and talking to the deceased. You may feel better, but their position hasn't changed. Literally!

TAKE TIME TO CHOOSE YOUR MATE

This time around, define your needs before meeting anyone. Assess the cost before beginning this journey. Ask yourself, 'What do I need, not want, in a mate?' What do you have to offer? Don't expect Denzel or Brad Pitt when you look like a Kraken sea monster! Be realistic. There is a fine line between having realistic expectations and accepting whatever comes your way. This time around, you know what you wish you knew then. Time and experience have changed you for the better. Your choices should be much wiser.

Decide if this is the right time for you to date. If you're not ready, spare yourself and someone else needless heartache. You are in no hurry. The last few months, weeks and days have been spent in a cocoon anyway. Think of it like this, if a butterfly left the incubation process too soon, what would happen? Would having extra feet and partially developed wings be a good thing? No! So take all the time you need to be that beautiful, full-formed creature you can be. He who began a great work in you will finish it. Don't start something you're not ready to finish. Timing is everything. Just because you're ready, the person God is sending you may not be. The universe knows what you need and when to give it to you. I caution you, don't try to bless yourself.

Struggling to meet someone new is unwise. Allow nature to take its course. Use the down time to prepare yourself. In the meantime, you have plenty of opportunities to refine yourself. Complete your education, get in better shape, clean your house or take a sabbatical are only a few suggestions. If you can't handle being alone with yourself, who else wants to be? Use this time to revamp your relationship expectations. Ask God to reveal more about you to yourself.

Get the preconceived notions out of your head about who your perfect partner is. Permit time to have its perfect work in your life. Have you ever noticed that when you stop looking, that's when a real opportunity for something special comes your way? What if that happens and you haven't adequately prepared yourself? Why would someone want you if you're not equally yoked with them? While you wait your turn, focus on things that truly make you happy. Perfect your gifts. Those are the same things that you have to share with the person who God is sending you.

Until your season comes, this provides the perfect opportunity to get rid of some old fears while building up some strengths. Anxious feelings about meeting someone new will subside when you are busy. Use this time to enrich your personality, fine-tune your communication skills and become more spiritually grounded. People are naturally attracted to those who are at peace with themselves. After all, nobody wants you to sap the energy from their world. If anything, they want you to invigorate them. Healthy co-dependence is a good thing; parasitic attachment is suffocating at best. It's good to need and be needed, not needy.

UNWRITTEN RULES TO DATING

Follow your instincts.

Gut feelings make all the difference in the world. Words, actions and gestures from other people create an instinctive response. The response can be good or it can set off an alarm. In a previous chapter I referred to these alarms as signs. These are things that your conscious mind misses, but your spirit picks up. I'm not referring to something as obvious as a woodsman's ax and hockey mask. I'm talking about being sensitive to your spirit, your gut instincts. If a potential date triggers your spirit's internal alarm system, heed it! It will do one of two things: Either it will keep you from prematurely dismissing a good person, or it will spare you from attaching yourself to another walking nightmare.

An example: You meet someone online. If their profile

says they're six foot two and athletic but you hear reindeer in the background and they ask you how you like green felt suits, this may not be a good idea. Okay, that's not what I'm talking about either. What I am referring to is something like this. During an online chat they seem interesting but after speaking with them you get a sense that something isn't quite right. It could be as subtle as the tone in the voice, something said, or even just a gut feeling. Bottom line: Heed the warning.

A more positive example would be an awkward date but something tells you next time will be better. The person could be nervous or between paychecks and didn't want to put off meeting you. Give the person a second chance. You could be missing out on a good thing.

Actions speak louder than words.

What people say is one thing, what they do is another. Out of the abundance of the heart the mouth will speak. Where a person's heart is, is where the put their treasure. Pay attention to the little things that people do, it speaks volumes!

<u>An example:</u> Someone treats you very well but consistently talks about other people in derogatory, condescending ways. Another red flag is that they can only engage you when inebriated. You're probably dealing with someone who won't make such good company under normal circumstances. There is a difference between game and charisma. Often shy people aren't smooth but that doesn't mean they're not good for you. The same is true for

confident personalities. Sometimes they appear arrogant on the surface, when in fact they are just very self-assured. In other words, judge the heart and its intentions. It takes the time to get to know a potential mate, but a key indicator of how they will treat you is how they treat others. Pay particular attention to how the person interacts with waiters, children and the elderly. I have found that to be a very good barometer for hidden traits. Another is to listen to a person's comments while viewing television programs or movies. That reveals attitudes and predispositions. People are stable over time.

Don't play games.

Life is not a television program. If someone gets shot in a television program, they get over it during the commercial break. In real life injured feelings don't heal so quickly. 'I'm sorry' or 'I won't do it again' gets old. People are human and they get tired of having the same immature, needless hurts occur repeatedly. Don't take people or their feelings for granted. People who are attempting to live a fulfilling life don't have time for emotional, attention- getting behaviors. Tell people the truth about your feelings. You will reap what you sow, so plant cautiously. Be honest, don't lead people on. If you aren't genuinely interested in a person, don't take their phone number or go out with them. Such behaviors are seen as leading someone on. If you aren't interested, communicate that in an honorable way.

Be polite, always thank the person for their interest. Tell

them you are flattered, but you must respectfully decline. Try using those exact words or something very similar. Do not say, 'Let me think about it,' 'Maybe later,' or 'Call me in a week.' That is just tacky and trifling. Tell the truth, let people down easy, and don' t play games. Know when to call it a day.

An example: If you are only interested in casual dating, say so. Never allow someone to believe they have an exclusive relationship with you when they don't. People end up with hurt feelings, get in fights and have even gotten killed over folks lying about relationships. Women and men are equally responsible for treating people the way they want to be treated. 'Do unto others as you would have them do unto you.' If have no intention of taking someone seriously, don't accept gifts, money or take trips with them. You are sending the wrong message and it's an implied endorsement. Both sexes hear what they want to hear if you don't stop it from happening. Even then some people don't know how to accept the 'no' for an answer. In such cases, you must cut off all contact with that person. That is a potential stalker!

If you are only interested in a serious relationship, tell the person up front. People who have a hidden agenda will hear you say you're only interested in something serious and then use you to get what they want. They will string you along just to get what they want, be it sex, money or a validated ego. A great deal of needless suffering can be avoided by seeking the truth when dealing with others. You cannot change someone's opinion of what they want. If the person that you think is perfect for you indicates there is no interest in a commitment, accept it! Manipulating, forcing or hoping they will change will result in your heart being broken. Respect their decision. This is especially true if you screwed up with them. Once trust is destroyed, it is difficult at best to get it back. Accept friendship and work on yourself. Don't delay the inevitable. In the end they will respect you for it and you will spare yourself much needless heartache.

Presentation is everything.

Be the best you. Putting your best foot forward requires consistent effort. Be more concerned about how you are in reality, not how you appear. It's true that appearance plays a major role in attraction because people are visual. But intelligent people use the mind's eye as much as the ones in their head. Character and integrity are the most important qualities you need. Looks get attention but a great personality and pleasant nature keep it.

'She looked good, until she opened her mouth. After that things got uglier by the second.' Talk about an accurate statement. Nothing is more attractive than a sincerely genuine person. The sexiest character trait is authenticity. This may sound like a silly suggestion, but I strongly suggest you see the movie 'Shrek.' It provides a humorous look at authenticity. Though an ogre, Shrek doesn't try to be anything other than himself and the result is that Shrek finds his true love in Fiona. Had he not been the farting, ill-mannered, non-conformist ogre God created him to be, never would he have found true love.

I'm not suggesting you go around farting, not bathing and abandon paying attention to your physical appearance. You aren't Shrek. However, it's important that you be the best you possible. To the best of your ability be the total package. Do looks matter? Unless you are totally desperate, the answer is 'Yes.' Personality and character are very important qualities but your mate has to look at you. Nobody wants to date a charismatic beast. You get one chance to make a good impression and that's each and every time your mate sees you. To do that, use everything God gave you. Mind, body and soul. Every time you see the person you're interested in, bring all of you to the table. If you begin with your game face on, then take it off every other moment, otherwise you may as well not wear it at all.

Imagine this: You haven't been out in months. After putting on your new shoes and new suit, you head to what you think will be a wonderful night on the town. Based on the commercial, the place looks fantastic. However, upon arrival, you get some bad impressions. A couple of lights in the restaurant's sign are out. You see a few dead insects in the window. You blow it off and go in. Ten minutes pass before anyone greets you. The waiter has a nonchalant attitude.

You consider leaving but you want to give the place a chance. Maybe things will get better. Finally, you get to your table and the table across from yours has dirty dishes on it; they remain there for the course of your visit. In an attempt to enjoy what is turning into a horrible evening, you order food. When you get your dinner, it's cold. After mulling over a plate of less than tasty food you ask where the rest room is. You find it; it's nasty. After returning to your seat, the bill is there waiting on you. How would that make you feel? Would you come back? More than likely, 'Hell no!'

External appeal may be great; nonetheless, if the quality isn't there you have nothing. As with this restaurant, your character must match your presentation. Both matter.

Be authentic.

A non-authentic person is the same as that restaurant. Possessing the quality is one thing, demonstrating it is another. How you are and how you look matter. You must be equally concerned about both. Being that which you seek is much more than a cliché, it must become a lifestyle. Deliberately acquire an image that you can maintain. Looking wealthy is one thing, being legitimately rich in character is another. Nothing beats being the real you, except packaging it well. It's okay to be a work in progress. All of us are.

Driving a $40,000 car and living in an apartment, wearing three hundred dollar shoes with fake jewelry, or getting your hair done every week and having no lunch money doesn't impress anyone. It makes you look like a fool. Shopping at Walmart or Neiman Marcus, doesn't make you who you are. You can be a Walmart shopper and have it going on; Neiman Marcus could wardrobe you from head to toe and you still will be one expensively dressed jerk. It's all in how you work it.

A great smile, charismatic personality and authenticity beats the heck out of a jerk in an Armani suit. Clothes enhance you, they don't make you. Take the time to study style. Find something that works for you. I'm not endorsing any store, but value-oriented stores like Ross, TJ Maxx, and the like, put decent fashion within the reach of the average person. The goal is to put your best foot forward at all times. No one will know if your outfit came from a thrift store or consignment shop.

<u>An example:</u> My family has every type of woman you could imagine. Spaghetti thin, big-boned, tall, short. You name it, we got it. So I don't upset anyone, but my two deceased relatives, they will be my examples. I had an aunt who was about five foot eleven, 120 pounds with lead underwear on. She had no butt and long beautiful hair. But she constantly wore short shorts, too much make up, and flat shoes. Needless to say, I am not a fashion designer. But my auntie looked a hot mess. The girl had something to work with but didn't know how to use it. On the opposite end of the spectrum, my sweetest aunt was about five foot one, 240 pounds. She had a nice butt, shoulders and no neck to speak of. She was pretty as you could get, but she often looked ridiculous in clothes that were too tight. Whatever your body type, put on something that extenuates your better features. Don't run around looking as though you have on your parent's clothes. Whether you're plus size or thin as a rail, work with what God gave you. Ask a real friend to give you an honest opinion. Some

people get a kick out of tripping off of you. More than likely if two or more people tell you something sucks on you, it does! Whatever your figure, someone will like you just the way you are.

Be sure that whatever you wear is clean and unwrinkled. Resist the temptation to go out of the house tattered, no matter how comfortable wearing your flannel pajamas and cartoon character house shoes to the store makes you feel. You never know whom you're going to meet or what opportunities will be in your path.

Cleanliness is next to Godliness.

If you are going on a date, clean your home and your car. Cheetos in the seat, junk in the floor, a nasty bathroom and or an odor in your refrigerator imply one of two things: you don't manage time well or you're nasty. This definitely applies to men and is especially true for women. Men, worth keeping, love a neat and orderly woman. The way you take care of your possessions implies that's the way you take care of yourself. No matter how much you apologize, it creates a poor impression.

FIVE BEHAVIORS THAT KEEP YOU SINGLE

The way you present yourself can raise or lower your score on a potential suitor's list. Any of the personalities below display over-the-top behaviors that will guarantee you remain single for a long time, if not the rest of your life.

- ◆ Chatty Kathy (or Ken)

- Party Animal
- Dependent Personality
- Commitment-phile
- Flirt
- Attention Freak

Blah, Blah, Blah, Yakkity Yak

A Chatty Kathy or Ken loves nothing more than hearing the sound of their own voice. If that's you, keep it up. That's one way to guarantee it will be the only voice you hear. Communication is a two-way process. How can you get to know a person if you don't shut up? Waiting to talk isn't listening. It is rude, offensive and people know when you are halfway listening to them. Think about the last time you were with someone who kept talking about themselves for minutes on end. Minutes turn to hours quickly under such circumstances. When you meet someone new, make an effort to hear what the person is actually saying and consider how you will respond. Create a dialog, not a monologue.

The Party Animal

Sane people aren't interested in an interspecies relationship. Being a party animal only benefits a club owner. It's okay to be the life of the party, even a ball of fun. Most people will gravitate to you when you're in a festive environment but that changes when it comes to someone taking you seriously. Nobody wants a wild person for a potential partner. Those qualities don't go well with parenting, meeting future in-laws or business colleagues. As a matter of fact, such character traits become intimidating. An outgoing personality and great dance moves are wonderful social skills as long as that's what they are. If those things are the core of your personality, I strongly urge you to expand your horizons. Being unable to amuse yourself without a mind-altering substance or environment is a very unattractive quality.

Mr. or Ms. Dependent

A person who can't stand on their own is a scary date. Men and woman agree that they want a partner who brings something to the table. Good looks, sex and money will take you so far, what else do you have to offer becomes much more significant over time. Calling someone fifteen times a day or flying off the handle when the other person is not within monitoring distance becomes burdensome. If you want to run someone off, be dependent. Clinging smothers any chance of being missed. This behavior is energy draining and exhausts a person's patience quickly.

The Commitment-phile

You've just met and fewer than twenty-four hours later, your new date considers it time for the wedding. I'm not talking about someone who has known or observed you for a length some time. The Commitment-phile is the person who met you online, had one date and is now busy making plans for nuptials. If you happen to meet someone who knocks your socks off, that's great. However, take your time and enjoy the process. Love at first sight does still happen but take the time to enjoy the process. Make sure you aren't projecting your desires on someone you barely know. The best relationships are built on a solid foundation and that takes time.

The Flirt

Flirts can seem attractive at first until things become serious and you consider settling down with them. After all, flirters make the 'getting to know you' aspect of dating effortless. Courtship is easier since the guessing games are eliminated. Unfortunately, this quality is why the flirty bird fails in serious relationships. Typically this person is seeking in other people what is missing in themselves and they have a subconscious need to control everyone in the room. But do you really want to be in a serious relationship with someone who is continually flirting with everyone? It raises the question of whether or not that person can truly commit to you in a monogamous relationship.

A situational flirt is different from a serial flirt. A situational flirt might simply have a good time at a party. If they learn that their behavior concerns you, and care about you, they can stop. The serial flirter cannot cut it off. They flirt out of convenience and habit. Major self-esteem issues are at the root of this behavior.

The Attention Freak

The Attention Freak is a drama addict who doesn't care if the attention is negative or positive. A good comparison is a child and a toy. The kid doesn't care about the toy until someone else wants it. These are people who typically hang on to non-productive relationships. Rather than engaging themselves with autonomous activities they depend on the other people for validation. If two people with this personality defect get involved it is an accident waiting to happen. Hobbies, education and social service provide healthy outlets for such needs.

COMMUNICATION SKILLS

What and how you communicate is the key to sending the right message to a potential mate. Talking is the smallest part of communication. Only 7% of communication is verbal; 38% is intonation and inflection in your voice. A firm or stern tone indicates authority; a shaky, uneven voice suggests nervousness. A person who knows how to control the tone, pitch and inflection in their voice has a much stronger potential to attract attention than someone that doesn't.

Gestures, body language and other non-verbal forms of communication are more important than words. Studies indicate that across cultural, gender, age and race, communication by gesture makes more of an impact than what a person says. It is imperative that you master the signals you send other people. This artful dance serves many purposes. Sending the right signals prevents unwanted advances and makes it possible for strangers to become comfortable with each other without saying a word.

It starts with the eyes. The eyes are the keys to the soul;

moreover, they make communicating much easier and the right look, at the right moment, makes a huge difference. Making or avoiding eye contact is a substantial part of non-verbal communication. Eye contact accompanied by a smile creates an open invitation for dialogue; the opposite is true when eye contact is accompanied by a stern or discontented facial expression.

Facial expressions either repel or invite people to engage you. A calm, inviting facial expression goes along way in social and professional environments. When it comes to dating, the look on your face will make or break you. The trick here is to simply be authentic. Be yourself. Your face will reflect your personality and say volumes. And learning to smile more often never hurt anyone.

Swagger is the term for the decade. The definition is to walk or behave in an overly confident, typically arrogant or aggressive manner. But how we walk, stand and look has a great deal to do with how we are perceived by others and says a lot about how we see ourselves. I suggest you get a full-length mirror and observe yourself. When you are in a public environment, discretely put yourself in a position to see your reflection. It will help you self-monitor yourself so you can pay attention to how you're standing and your facial expressions.

Techniques to maximize your physical presence:

- When greeting someone, smile.
- Don't invade other people's personal space; typically that's eighteen inches away.

- Listen more than you talk, especially when meeting someone for the first time or when you are in crowd.

- Don't stare, but keep eye contact.

- Look in a mirror prior to going out in public; check your nose and teeth for foreign objects.

- Touch people sparingly; it's better that you allow them to touch you first.

- Think before you talk.

- Know your place in a social group; if you're new to the group, speak when spoken to; even then, don't talk to much.

- Mirror the facial expressions of those you speak with.

Effective use of body language makes you more attractive; moreover, it is the first step in providing insights into who you are without your saying one word. As with any social grace it requires practice, but it is well worth the effort. Whether your communication goal is personal or professional, authenticity is key. There is nothing simple about you and keep that in mind when you deal with other people. They have an agenda just like you do and it takes time to get to know why people are present in your life. Examine your motivations and theirs. Make sure that you sincerely have each other's interest at heart. Then enjoy the process of getting to know people and take your time. Remember that you are not meant to fit with everyone. After all, that's exactly what makes a good relationship special. When you meet the right person, be it a friend, professional associate or potential mate, honesty, character and integrity are the keys to quality.

CHAPTER 9

YES, I'M SINGLE

GETTING BACK IN THE DATING GAME AND WINNING

Single, ready to mingle? You may ask: 'How do I meet the right person?' Pickup lines, pheromones, being sexy, and flirting techniques may work if you're looking for Mr. or Mrs. Right Now. But, if you're looking for something more fulfilling, you need something better. Being a pickup artist is one thing, getting to know the right someone, having them develop a genuine interest in you is another.

Lasting relationships are based on finding quality, not quantity. Using the right approach is key in meeting the right person Using the right approach is key in finding a potential mate and avoiding rejection. The next step is distinguishing yourself from the group while capturing a potential mate's attention. Knowing what to say, when and how to say it, mingling, good timing, and demonstrating social skills positions you to meet and keep the right person's attention. It takes less than one minute for dialogue and presentation to make or break you.

The first step is dating is finding the right person and locating him or her is equivalent to fishing a certain type of fish. Successfully catching the right fish is a matter of timing, going to the right spot and using the proper bait. Your goal should not be based on the quantity, but the quality of potential suitors. Meeting a group of playboys, spinsters or bar flies is a waste of time. If your next relationship is going to work you need to know what you want and truly deserve in a partner. Too much time has been invested in yourself to settle for anything less than a quality match. 'Be careful what you ask for, you might get it.' Attracting the wrong person, sabotaging a potential relationship, and having difficulties maintaining a good relationship happen for one reason—reacting and not thinking before you act. Thriving love connections are a direct result of being proactive.

Earlier in life, my relationship needs were very superficial. My checklist started with measurements, attractiveness, education and income. Little, if any, thought was given to what I needed in a mate. That required having patience. Like most immature people, I was attracted to body parts, not character traits. They were successful, well educated, and the sex was great; nonetheless, I couldn't find a love connection to save my life. As time passed, I kept wondering why I had repeatedly met very attractive women, but not one suited me nor kept my interest. Finally, I figured my problem out. I was getting what my eyes liked, but not what my heart and head needed. I had to stop blaming the women and take a good look at what I was doing wrong. Back to my fishing analogy, you can't catch marlin with a catfish mentality. I had to redefine what I was looking for. That led me to examining what my long, not short term, priorities were. Then I had to change my approach toward obtaining my goal. Another way to think about this is: how can you catch what your looking for, especially if you keep using the wrong tackle? Moreover, how are you going to be able to keep it even if you get what you're looking for? Marlin won't fit in the holding tank. Come prepared, you must be what you seek.

Discard those old mental dating maps. Those out-dated charts facilitated the last botched journey to love land. A bad choice of lures drew the wrong people your way. You'll use a different strategy this time. You will be the bait, not the fisher. Authenticity, sincerity and character are your new calling cards. Great, lasting relationships are based on common interest, shared values, likened principals and morals. What is important to you? Is it great sex, financial security, and good looks? Or, are you finally mature enough to realize that true love, someone to share ups and downs, means that commitment and integrity matter, too.

Success at anything requires time and preparation. Good relationships are the result of intention.

'You receive not, because you ask not.' I wanted the complete package in a woman, but I kept using body parts as the criteria. Typically, I succeeded in getting what I sought in a woman. Nonetheless, I am to be honest, I was settling and didn't know it. I put the emphasis on what I wanted and didn't take the time to consider what I needed. Adding insult to injury, my game plan and approach were wrong. Several mistakes were made. One, I focused on the external qualities, not realizing that personality, morals and character were equally as important as beauty. Two, I needed to look in different places if was going to meet the type of woman I desired in my life. Three, I didn't let time to work in my favor. Last but not least, I tried to bless myself. I forgot God could give me what I wanted and needed in a mate. The definition of relationship is two people who are connected. It's easy to hook up with people, but you cannot connect with everyone.

Quality takes time. Now is the time to know what you seek in a mate. Stop wishing, and start willing the right people into your life. Ironically this starts with you. Write down your best qualities. Ask yourself, 'If I could change something about me what would it be?' What are you going to revamp about yourself that will make attracting the right person easier? Start with the things that are easy to change such as your style of dress, hair, personality, and attitude.

How would you reinvent your lifestyle? Set a time frame to make those internal and external adjustments. Last, but not least, accept the fact that you are a diamond in the rough. Communicate that to the people you meet. Water finds its level.

Describe what you need in a companion. Define what those attributes are and what they mean to you. Are you ready to commit to finding and keeping that which you seek? It's not difficult to attract the right person to your life. Being that which you seek is the first step.

During this season, do your homework. Every city has a weekend events section in the newspaper. Use that to expand your horizons. Go where the sort of people you want to meet hang. This may be a bit awkward at first. Think of it as a vacation. It would shock you how many people live in a city and know so little about it. Be prepared for rejection, some people may be in the same physical place you are, but they are in a totally different place mentally.

No matter where you go, what you do or how good you look, everybody is not going to appreciate you. Not everyone is resurrecting themselves like you are. So as you get ready to begin this journey, be prepared for people who are where you just left mentally and emotionally. Thank God for that! Relationships are special, not generic. Nothing is more rewarding than meeting people who are at the same place you are inwardly. The trick here is enjoy the moment, but be alert.

Success in love will sneak up on you. The definition of success is: preparation meeting opportunity. Typically you will develop a lasting meaningful bond with someone under the most common of circumstances. God tailor-makes such situations for you.

The difference between an idea and a goal is a 'date.' In the meantime, you need to do some things differently. Plan three things every day that move your life in a fulfilling direction with the goal of preparing yourself for love. I have a few suggestions.

If you change these five things you will greatly enhance your chances of meeting suitable people:

- Start attending cultural events—plays, museums, festivals.

- Get out more—go to the park, the beach, ride a bike, walk, skate.

- Take your butt back to church or simply Zen out on a regular basis (if you already do that, get active, don't be a bench member) and nourish your spirit.

- Give back to the community—volunteer time with the elderly, at a homeless shelter, food bank or get involved with kids in your community.

- Listen to live music—upwardly mobile people love live music: jazz, concerts and the symphony.

It's time to start putting your life in order. We're done getting over that old relationship. After trying different things, by now, you should know what works for you. Let's enjoy meeting new people, for the sake of enhancing your circle of friends. The difference is, this time, we are going to do that the right way. Do some people-watching, take your time observing people's traits. Spot traits that you wish to emulate as well as those you need to abandon.

This is the perfect time to spot qualities you seek in a partner. The key to a successful relationship specifically begins with observing what turns you on when it comes to other people. Take notice of what you need and want. Now make a list.

Here are some areas to consider:

- ◆ Values systems, Morals and Principals—revealed by observing how people treat their relatives, friends and community (this especially includes ex-lovers and ex-spouses)
- ◆ Lifestyle—indicated by places an individual frequents, the social groups and activities they pursue
- ◆ Commitment—observing how someone consistently cares for children, pets, themselves and others is a great indicator for the level of potential faithfulness

Next we are going to define what you want in a partner:

- ◆ Determine what type of personality you are drawn to.
- ◆ Determine positive activities that you enjoy doing on a regular basis.
- ◆ Review your weaknesses, the things you need someone to balance. For example, if you aren't good as socializing, perhaps you need someone who is better at it and can draw you out.

- List habits that you are not willing to tolerate.
- List activities that you are not willing to give up.
- Consider which personality traits are a deal breaker.
- Even better, consider which personality traits are a deal maker.

This is your core value system. Before meeting, dating or committing to anyone, realize these traits are your idiosyncrasies. It's the little things that make or break relationships. An ounce of prevention beats a pound of cure.

Now's the time to be very honest with yourself. You, and any potential mate, must take these valuable considerations into account. Leopards and zebras do not change their spots or stripes and neither will you. Create a list from the information you wrote down. Keep it with you. If you don't, you will regret it. You will use it one day, trust me. It's a Cliff Notes version of you.

The next step is putting yourself in environments to meet people who possess the traits and personality characteristics you desire.

Examples: Most people with a healthy concern for what is right and wrong go to church (remember, correlation doesn't infer causation). People who are compassionate volunteer their time to help social organizations. Health-conscious people walk, ride bikes and go to the gym on a regular basis. Folks who enjoy the arts attend plays, museums and festivals.

Once you find the right environment, you will encounter people who share your interest. The next step is getting the right person's attention.

Flirting, by definition, is deliberately exposing yourself to or showing a superficial interest in someone. Sending and receiving cues is the essential in meeting a potential mate. In the past, typically, we flirted with people based on that superficial surface attraction. This time we are going to take a different approach.

Flirting is the time to show off your best features. It's about creating value and communication. How you communicate your interest is paramount. I suggest starting with a smile, pleasant demeanor and being approachable. Overt behavior is an extreme turn-off. Both men, and women typically resort to sex appeal, dressing to impress or showing off assets (jewelry, cars, physical features and money) to get someone's attention. I caution you to remember this. Whatever you do to get someone's attention, that is what you more than likely will have to do to keep it. Using things to attract someone is foolish and a sign of insecurity. You're setting yourself up to be taken advantage of. There will always be someone more attractive, with more money, jewelry and stuff. But nobody can replace your integrity or character. Those things are priceless.

Unless your goal is to be a sex worker, this isn't about perfecting the art of flirting. Flirting isn't a talent nor is it a skill; it is something you do to get the attention of someone who sincerely interests you. The way you conduct yourself, your charisma and a pleasant demeanor are your calling cards. The first step in getting attention is creating impressions and making a positive impact. Your goal is to be noticed by the right person, not everyone. You don't want to seem desperate.

Looking your best says volumes about you. Well-kept people send two messages. 1) You take care of, and care about yourself. 2) You can enhance someone else. Men and women are attracted to classy not trashy presentations. This is the time to be authentic. Never put forth an image that cannot be maintained. If you can't wear a $500 suit everyday, don't try to. Nothing beats being yourself, the trick is consistently being the best you possible. Always wear something that is cleaned, pressed and in style. It doesn't have to be expensive.

Eye contact is the first sign of interest. Use your eyes to probe for interest. Showing someone that you are excluding everyone and everything in a room creates a thrill for the person you are looking at. Make sure that you are serious; if you do this with more than one person you will alienate them. You never know who knows whom. Nonetheless, if you do this a couple of times you will catch someone's eye. Depending on your style, either be bold, or gaze and look away. Do what works for you.

Give people time to react. Acting like a bull in the china shop is never a wise approach. Allow enough time to pass for the person to respond to your glance. This prevents you from looking like a fool or hitting on someone else's mate.

If the interest is mutual, the person more than likely will return the gesture or may approach you. If they are shy, get proximal to them. Say hello and introduce yourself. People don't like rejection so in many instances they want to make sure that you're really checking them out. Whatever the case, 'Hello' and introducing yourself is the appropriate way to meet anyone. Next pay attention to the person's name. Don't forget it. The sweetest sound to someone's ears is the mention of their name. It demonstrates that you are paying attention.

Your conversation is the biggest factor in gaining the interest of another person. What you talk about and how it's presented reflects your attitudes, intellect, education and level of compassion. Within a few minutes your presentation reveals a great deal about you. Nobody is attracted to a fool except an idiot. Think before you speak. Don't wait to talk, listen to what is being said to you. Don't imitate, but mirror the other person's gestures and facial expressions.

Ten fool-proof topics add value to your conversation:

- Say something relevant about the environment you're in.

- Ask how long the person's lived here.

- Talk about recent movies, cultural events or restaurants.

- Ask for opinions or suggestions about something.

- Pay a compliment.

- Ask, 'May I join you?'

- Make a comment about the weather.
- Tell a joke.
- Ask where the person went to school.
- Never discuss politics, family or religion.

Get to know people. An opinion opener is a great way to start a dialog. But what you do after that will make or break you. This isn't a time to tell your life history, but is the perfect time to ask open-ended questions. The goal is to listen twice as much as you talk. Your goal is to passively pick up on preferences, attitudes and opinions. Never let someone feel as though you're giving them the third degree. If they have friends present, include them in the conversation. You can learn a lot by observing their interactions. Pay close attention to reactions and statements made. They provide insight into latent behaviors.

Be attentive. The goal is not to get attention, it's to demonstrate value. Nobody throws away good people. Both sexes appreciate your valuing their time. It implies that you aren't taking them for granted. Include everyone in the conversation. This will show you how interested a person is in you. Also, you want the person's friends to get a good impression of you.

Be considerate. That doesn't mean becoming Mr. or Mrs. Congeniality. But, be sensitive to your environment. Don't stand closer than an arm's length to someone unless they come to closer to you. Don't be rude to their friends. By including everyone in the conversation you demonstrate good social aptitude. Acknowledge that you don't want to intrude, don't wear out your welcome. After a few moments pass, ask the person that you are interested in whether you may speak with them for a moment. This demonstrates that you respect boundaries. When one on one, ask the big question, 'Are you dating someone or in a relationship?' If they say yes, stop! You will reap what you sow. If you're looking for a serious relationship, you are setting yourself up for failure. Not to mention, if they do that, down the road you will not be able to trust them. However, if they are single, ask if you may contact them later. Don't be pushy. Offer to give them your number, allow them time to voluntarily give you theirs.

Putting your best foot forward is a good thing, just use your head. Remember, this is about being the real you. If you want to be happy, allow people to like you for who you are, not a façade. Nobody loves a caricature or a charlatan. Nothing beats the real you. Nobody is perfect and you don't have to be. This is about demonstrating your value, not how cool you are.

Here are a few things that you can do that require little if any effort on your part. Commit this list to memory:

- Be nice. Kindness doesn't cost you a thing. People are attracted to sincere authentic people. Being considerate not only makes you stand out, it makes someone miss you when you're not there.

- Treat other people the way you wish to be treated. 'Do unto others as you would have them do unto you.' Mindful acts seldom go unnoticed. Making sure someone got in safe, reminding them of appointments or an encouraging word goes along way.

◆ Good hygiene is sexy. Stay well groomed. Keep your hair, nails and skin in good condition. Nobody is attracted to a stinky person with bad breath. Self-monitoring is a good thing as long as you don't take it to an extreme.

◆ Dress for the occasion. If you're going to the grocery store, dinner or park, dress appropriately.

◆ Use your sex appeal. Let your best features show. It may be your voice, sharp wit or intellect. Use what God gave you.

◆ Show off the features your mate likes most. The trick here is do the right thing at the right time. You want your significant other to feel special. If they like your legs, lips or eyes, then do or wear something that accentuates them. Make the most of your best features. If you've got it flaunt it the right way, at the right time.

It takes eight hours to build or sabotage rapport. During that time the object of your affection is either putting you in the lover, friend or weirdo category. Seldom does that eight hours take place at one time. Typically it happens over a couple of dates and a few phone conversations. Things said and done in those moments will make or break you. If you are truly interested in the person, make the time to date. Build attraction by creative engagements. Nothing beats going for coffee, a walk in the park, or visiting the zoo. Make yourself part of the environment. Avoid nightclubs, restaurants, and visiting friends or relatives. Those sets distract. The goal is to increase the focus on each other. Commercial settings typically will hinder, not aid your efforts in getting to know one and other.

Playing it cool, posturing and stalling makes you look insecure, uninterested or ill at ease. People need to feel wanted. This is especially true if the person you're attracted to is successful, attractive or in a demanding profession. They can quickly shift attention to other people, priorities or work. To whom much is given, much is required. You are not the only person who noticed them, believe that. Don't take your good find for granted. Another way to look at this is, pretend you found a diamond in the street. If you set it down on a table in a crowded restaurant, how long would it take for someone else to spot it? One person's trash is another's treasure.

Quality people are busy. Don't get miffed if they take a few hours or even a day to return your call. Successful folk aren't sitting around waiting on the phone to ring. It is not unusual for a professional to put in twelve-hour days; a small business owner is typically wearing a minimum of three hats; a single parent has to juggle transporting kids, going to work and taking care of home at the very least. Being mindful of their needs strengthens your position. Supportive gestures make you a valued addition as opposed to a pain in the butt.

Here are a few things that you can do to bring positive attention to yourself:

- Ask if there is anything you can do to be of assistance.
- Be on time: that is the uttermost sign of respect.
- Provide a listening ear.
- Be the voice of reason, but pick your moments.
- Offer to pick up a meal, dry cleaning or run an errand.
- Offer a retreat at your home, a hotel or day spa.
- Cook dinner.
- Buy something functional for the kids—pizza, learning toy, gift certificates.
- Help maintain their vehicle—carwash, gas, cleaning the interior.
- Assist with domestic duties—offer to help do simple house chores, yard work etc.
- Show sensitivity to pets and their needs—feeding, grooming, walking.

Those things do not cost a lot of money, they require your time. Self-sufficient people don't need your loot, they need your support. Kind gestures go much further than trinkets, flattery, sex or money. The issue here is don't do anything with an ulterior motive. Whatever you do, be sincere. Make sure it comes from the heart. People can tell when you're manipulating them. Hidden agendas always reveal themselves. Consistency is key. Don't do anything that you cannot keep up. If this relationship grows, whatever you did to get your significant other's attention will need to be maintained to keep their interest.

Last but not least, charm works. Though many things have changed in culture, good manners, etiquette and poise are valued qualities. Speaking softly, being courteous and sensitive to the concerns of others sets you apart from the average person. It demonstrates you're not just another face in the crowd. Virtue and class give you a distinguished persona, it reflects that you are not part of the rank and file. Such attributes make up for what you might lack in looks, wealth and education.

Remember, some people are better by nature than others are by practice, so go the extra mile. Not only will your prospective mate take notice, but those traits will open doors for you in other areas.

This is a time to be patient. Perfect being you while you wait for the right person to come in your path. Though you may be ready, God could still be grooming them. When it's the right time, that which you seek will be seeking you. Until then, work on you, and enjoy being single!

CHAPTER 10

LOVE IS

UNDERSTANDING, FINDING, AND KEEPING TRUE LOVE

Previously, I stated that love is the only game two can play and both lose. I also pointed out that love isn't a game. Confusing, but so is love. For some people love is an abstract concept, to others it is an ineffable feeling of attraction to another person, and to many more, it is a pleasurable sensation associated with a person, place or thing.

In years past the question of the day was, who do you love? Today, we need to ask ourselves, what do you love; moreover, why do you love it? What's love got to do with it? Everything! If you are to possess love, you must understand it. How can you keep something that you cannot comprehend? The key to being successful at love is deciphering it. The goal of this chapter is to teach you how to identify, accept, and develop love and be loved in return.

One definition of love is that it is a number of emotions related to a sense of strong affection and attachment. Another definition is that it is a deep feeling of romantic or sexual closeness to someone. I believe that love is ineffable, that it cannot be explained by speech. By that I am suggesting love is incomprehensible. It is inherently a complex proposition the escapes the boundaries of definition and is filled with paradoxes, impossibilities and boundless potentials. Most of us associate Love with a deep feeling of tenderly caring for another person, place or thing. I caution you, don't be so naive. Love is a power. It encompasses many dimensions, stages and definitions. It cannot be destroyed, it does not die, but it surely can elude you. If you respect it, you will be rewarded; if you honor it, it will honor you; if you play with it, you will lose. Love doesn't love anybody.

Romantic love is typically expressed with words or deeds. Conveyed by heightened feelings of excitement, sex and passion that are not handled properly, romantic love can result in emotional mutilation, physiological devastation and even suicide. It brings to life the statement, 'If you play with fire, you might get burned.' Love, like fire, can either comfort you, consume everything you have, blind you, or illuminate your path. This chapter is dedicated to teaching you how to handle the fire.

Love's Four Basic Categories

- Love based on Security
- Friendship Love
- Romantic, Erotic Love
- Unconditional Love

Security is the state of being free from threat. Being loved gives one a sense of protection, freedom from danger and a sense of invulnerability. Don't confuse romance and eroticism with love. Romance and eroticism are selfish constructs and have nothing to do with long-term balance and peace. Adults and children enjoy a purpose-filled existence because they have secure, unconditional love in their life. But, as with promiscuous adolescents, looking for love in all the wrong places for all the wrong reasons will get you played. People will tell you what you want to hear if it results in their getting what they want from you. It is not unusual for people to attempt to validate themselves in a pseudo love affair. When the bliss-filled moment is over, they end up worse off than before, with the only thing to show for it an STD, diminished reputation and added emotional scars. Typically this takes place because they are trying to find security via an illusion of love.

A truly secure love relationship can only exist between yourself and someone who is totally honest, open and comfortable. This is the basis for friendship love. Friendship love is a major component in forming enduring personality traits. In children it fosters unselfish acts, sharing and compassion; in adults camaraderie, dependability and character are proven when friendship love is tested. Loyalty, fidelity, honor and integrity are the fruits of friendship love. When tested they prove your sincerity and commitment. For a true love relationship to happen, friendship love must withstand pressure and challenge to demonstrate its validity.

Romantic love is seldom what it's titled. Romanticism and true romance are two different things. Real romantic love happens after a true relationship has been established. It is based on knowing the entirety of someone, their flaws, shortcomings, and imperfections and their knowing the same about you, and, despite that, remaining devoted to a progressing relationship—whereas romanticism is the shell of being romantic. Typically that mirage is misinterpreted as romance. It is the equivalent of looking at a Hyundai from a distance and assuming it's a Rolls Royce. Contrary to popular opinion, true romantic love only happens once, maybe twice in a lifetime. It takes time, hard work and commitment to establish a true romantic relationship.

Don't mistake these emotions with love:

- ◆ Infatuation—inspired with an intense, but short-lived passion or admiration
- ◆ Affection—mental state based on a feeling of fondness or liking
- ◆ Lust—very strong sexual craving based on imagination or a sexual desire rooted in a need for validation or horniness
- ◆ Puppy Love—an intense but shallow romantic

attachment, typically associated with adolescents or immature people

- ◆ Temporary Comfort offered by ex-lovers, drugs and alcohol, none of which are good for you
- ◆ Work-related Relationships
- ◆ Adulterous Affairs

Avoid such situations. In the end, you'll have much more regret than satisfaction. Allow patience to have its perfect work in you. Good things come to those who wait.

Unconditional love is the sincere love that lasts forever. This type of love overcomes arguments, separation, finances, and anger. Nothing can destroy unconditional love. However, it doesn't just happen; it results from refinement, intention and commitment.

The desire to connect with another person, can lead to a long-term, fulfilling relationship or result in a traumatic experience that scars you for life. A large component of romantic love is Eros love—known as 'erotic love'—based on strong feelings of attraction for one toward each other. Usually occurring in the early stages of a relationship, Eros is largely based on physical traits.

Examples:

- ◆ A man falls in love with a woman based on her appearance.
- ◆ A woman is attracted to a man because of his ability to provide.
- ◆ Attractions that form at work due to appreciation

of one's position in an organization.

♦ Being smitten because of a person's success.

♦ Being charmed by charisma.

♦ Self benefit—what this person can do for you in times of need.

♦ Shared peril—two people in dysfunctional relationships having an affair.

♦ Being attracted to body parts—nice butt, breast, muscles.

♦ Someone's lifestyle.

Romantic and erotic love are relative terms. Both are generally accepted as moments and situations that develop during interpersonal situations. Since they are based on emotions, convenience, proximity, and the appearance of appreciation, romantic and erotic love are fleeting at best.

The obvious weakness in romantic and erotic love is its basis in self-benefit. It's rooted in 'feeling good' and making 'me' happy so often no real substance exists. The core is nothing more than an emotional high! Thus the term, 'falling in love.' To fall into something requires tripping, i.e., you are really 'tripping' if you think romance or eroticism is going to last. It won't. Love based on feelings alone will never work. How can it, if you haven't taken the time to really get to know who the other person really is? Feelings alone cannot be called 'real love.' Feelings, like moods, change according to circumstances.

During work, dates, social events and parties, people

always put their best foot forward, showing their best side. You are not going to have a waiter, empty office, or convention going on when you engage day-to-day life with someone. The grass always looks greener on the other side, until you have to mow it. In order to establish sincere connections with people you have to get to know and accept their good, and bad, traits. Dealing with time, joys, pain, pleasures and sorrows creates the foundation for a solid relationship. Untested love doesn't last. Too succeed at intimacy you have no choice but to reveal the real you to other people. Conversely, you must accept the flaws of other people. Real romances require give and take. Romantic and erotic love will only succeed if it evolves into a higher form: friendship.

Philos love, a love based on friendship, creates a state of mutual trust and support between two people. The cornerstone of a worthwhile significant partnership is based on the assurance that you can have confidence in it. Emotional maturity is necessary to experience such a relationship. A major part of friendship is the capability to love. Eradicating jealousy, pride and control issues is a direct result of sincere concern for another's well-being and success.

The advantage of starting out as friends is that you get to know each other. Solid foundations are based on a couple's getting to know each other for the right reasons. Then possibly, over time, genuine attraction and strong emotions can develop. As it relates to love, men are susceptible to youth and beauty, whereas many women seek status and security in a mate. Emotional maturity is the degree to which a person is capable of providing good treatment in a loving relationship.

Erotic and romantic love sees only each other's good side. Everything seems sexy, rosy and blissful. That is not reality. You cannot judge real love based on a mirage. If all your interactions involve liquor, a restaurant, club, sex, or even church, it will not work. Sooner, or later you will have to take off the veil and deal with the real person. A major disappointment happens when you attempt to interact with a real person as opposed to the caricature with whom you share you illusion. Disillusionment kicks in when you realize you are in love with a situation, not a person.

Philos, or friendship, is based on reciprocity between people. The foundation requires the type of give and take that benefits both people in order to form a genuine relationship—otherwise, what you have isn't authentic. People need to know that you are there for them and you need to know that they're there for you. As both parties give and receive in this process, your relationship develops more. Real love is a process. Allowing time to play its part in your relationship increases the meaning and value of your connection. You don't have to rush or demand things to have fulfillment. Often, God has given you exactly what you need; you just didn't take the time to see it. Your real friends aren't always going to agree with you, especially when you're wrong. They will support you when you don't believe in yourself. Friendship love causes you to grow.

Being friendly versus truly being friends is a huge difference. Real friends give without expecting anything in return. God showed us the best example of this by giving His ultimate gift and all He asks in return is that we love and appreciate Him for doing so. The same is true for you. Your real friends only want you to be the best you and they hurt when you're not. They love you unconditionally.

Unconditional love—agape love—is the highest type of love and is far superior to erotic or romantic love. Unconditional love is selfless, unmitigated, complete, and absolute. If you ever experienced it you probably cried. I did. Whether it is returned or not, the love is ever present.

EXAMPLES OF AGAPE LOVE

Say you mistreat your mother, but despite your behavior she continues to feed, clothe and put a roof over your head. Every day she says, 'I love you.'

If your parents are dying, you change their diapers, drive for hours to do their shopping, miss work just to comfort them, and expect nothing in return.

You have to take care of an infant but after you have worked for twelve hours, had little rest and you're tired as hell, the baby has a bad cold and fever. You stay up all night, cuddling, feeding and soothing the infant.

You're a sinner. Every day you do something to someone that is needless and causes them pain. But, despite yourself, God loves you. He gives you another chance the next day to get it right.

God wants you to be happy, so don't settle for less. You are capable of receiving and giving unconditional love. If you expect a miracle, you will get one. What you see in yourself others will see in you. Most of us wouldn't spot love if it walked up and bit us.

Stay on track by using this checklist as a daily reminder:

- Love is patient
- Love is kind
- Love does not envy
- Love does not boast
- Love is not proud
- Love is not rude
- Love is not self-seeking
- Love is not easily angered
- Love keeps no record of wrongs
- Love does not delight in evil
- Love rejoices in the truth
- Love always protects
- Love always trust
- Love always hopes
- Love always perseveres

The only person you can control is yourself, but I urge you to look for the traits above in other people. Seldom will you see all of them manifested at one time. Nonetheless, if you see your potential mate exhibit at least three of them a day you may have found the right person for you.

Remember, you must be that which you seek. Love is a choice. Love is a decision. Love is a state of being. Love is power. God is Love.

ACKNOWLEDGEMENTS

With thanks to the Reality -N- 3D Publishing, Inc. team, Leda, Nicole, Sakera, Andrenetta and AJ, my editor Rosanne, my CPA/attorney Ann, my layout artist Dania, and my Graphic Arts Director Carlos. Dear friend Gary, my frat Aaron, and my pastor Rudy, thanks for keeping my moral compass heading north. I love and appreciate all of you so much.